When Good
is not
Good Enough

When Good
is not
Good Enough

W. Scott Johnson

XULON PRESS

Xulon Press
2301 Lucien Way #415
Maitland, FL 32751
407.339.4217
www.xulonpress.com

Unless otherwise indicated, Scripture quotations taken from the King James Version (KJV) – *public domain.*

Printed in the United States of America.

ISBN-13: 978-1-6322-1095-1

To the Savior of my life, the Lord Jesus Christ and the leading of the Holy Spirit to write this book. Without Him, my life would be forever lost.

To my wonderful wife, Paula, for being the Christian spouse I needed to push me to a deeper walk with the Lord. I also thank her for living with an engineer for thirty-four years and making sure I made it safely home over thousands of bike rides.

To my mother, Connie Johnson, for being the super Christian influence throughout my life without who I would likely never have found and lived in the service of Jesus Christ

My grandfather, James Stevens (now deceased), for being more than just a Baptist minister, but a living a Christian example who put his faith into practice by helping others in times of need. Especially his investment in me.

Contents

Introduction

I f you are reading these words, you are likely standing in a bookstore in the religious section. If you are like most people, the title or the cover of this book caught your attention, so you picked it up and started scanning the first few pages... just to see if you might like it. This is very close to the old saying about judging a book by its cover. Now that you've read this far, I hope you got a brief chuckle and thought to yourself, "He's right." You might also be saying, "What a crazy way to start a book." So, keep reading a little further.

This book is not written by a prolific writer or famous author. In fact, it is the first publicly offered book I have ever written. Thank goodness I have an engineering degree to pay for my life's expenses. This book is the product of a person who just passed English and composition classes in college. However, I am really good at math. The editors really had to work on this one.

If the title of this book was what caught your attention, I hope that you consider reading further, to the conclusion. I consider this crucial information to pass along to readers. It was written to cause you to think about our existence and what happens to us when this life is over. If you decide to read this book, you will discover that it is not a deep, theological study of life after death, nor is it another book on near-death experiences. There are already plenty of books to cover those topics. This book only has a single purpose – to make you contemplate on what might happen next.

Being an engineer, I wanted this book to be short, simple, and to the point with a little humor added throughout the contents. There is no intention of coercing you into believing the way I do about what it means to be a good person. Each of us must come to some level of decision about what we believe when we near the end of our life on earth.

As you read this book, I hope you will be able to relate to some of the sections and compare the situation with events from your own life. My purpose is to take you along a typical life's journey and talk about the different phases each one of us grows through, with a focus on the last phase. I hope that, by this point you are asking yourself the question, *What do the phases of our life have to do with the title of this book?* There is a direct connection; trust me.

Let's take a walk through life...

Chapter 1

Life Phases

I grew up on a farm back in the 1970s. We really didn't have a lot of material things. Everything we did on the farm was achieved through manual labor. This was because my brother, sister, and I were cheap labor – or at least that was my perspective. We had lots of animals, several acres of farmland for crops, barns, tractors, and equipment, which meant lots of work. On a farm, there's never a day when you have no work to be done. Leisure time just didn't exist for our family. No matter what our age, from the time we could walk and stay safe, there was always some chore waiting.

As I reflect on my life, those early years on the farm were extremely valuable. Many life lessons can be learned on a farm, especially those that can get you into trouble. Oh, by the way, you do get really dirty on a farm, Mike Rowe should have done one of his *Dirty Jobs* shows on our farm.

Now, with nearly sixty years of experience living in our modern society, I want to take you back through the years of my life (and yours). My story may differ than yours as society, and technology in general, has changed significantly over my lifetime.

Regardless of where or how you grew up, we all, for the most part, go through the same phases of life.

While the individual events in each of these phases will be different, you will find many similarities. Those events shape the person you are today. I hope this little journey brings back some good memories of your life. Remember those, as you will need to recall them later in this book. Let's take a journey.

Baby Phase

The first phase in life is pretty obvious. It is those years from the moment of your birth up to about the point when you start school. You are totally dependent on everyone else to provide everything in life you need to survive. You didn't choose your parents, you didn't choose where you lived, you didn't choose what you wore for clothes, and you didn't even choose what you ate, for the most part. About all we do the first two years is eat and poop (yes, I used the word *poop* in a religious book, sorry to offend any of you out there).

How many of you had parents who took the traditional "naked baby/kid" picture? Then Mom would put a piece of tape over "certain parts" and stick it in the photo album only to have that picture pulled out to show your first boyfriend or girlfriend. Yes, my mom did that, too! My baby picture was taken back when you had to take a roll of film to the store, and they sent it off to have it developed, then the store returned your pictures in an envelope. That means there is some old photo developer out there who saw me as a baby in the buff. Don't laugh; there are several of you in the same boat.

During these early years, almost everyone around you is in control of your life. Even though you were not in control, this is one of the most critical times of your existence because this is the time you were learning and beginning to shape the person you would be in the years to come. This was also a time in your life when you had very little responsibility. The cares of life were not yours. All you were doing is learning to walk, talk, and open things that you shouldn't. The first words you spoke were *oh, so cute* to the adults around you, and it didn't take very long for those same adults a few months later to wish you would be quiet. From these very early years, you began to realize the difference between right and wrong. It's a little hard to understand, but we all had some way of knowing right and wrong already inside of us – even before we had help from the adults around us. Do you remember the first time someone told you "No," or said, "Don't do that"? We learned very quickly how to get away with breaking the rules and how to become sneaky.

During these early years, you that are older likely watched what I want to call *real cartoons* like Road Runner, Yosemite Sam, Popeye, and of course, Scooby Doo. You that are younger, most likely played digital learning games and believed in Santa Claus. You got to play T-ball, youth soccer, little league basketball, and learned to ride a bike and swim. Life was so simple and mostly fun. Then things began to change.

My wife has worked in child care for most of her life, and the last several years, she has run a large daycare at our local church. I get to hear all about how the behavior of children is growing increasingly worse as the years pass. If you don't want something told in public, then do not say it in front of your kids and take them to daycare. Children learn and repeat what happens in their homes. My wife should write a book about the Life and Times of a Daycare Worker.

One specific story my wife told me was about a child that, at the age of three, could already drop the "F bomb" and knew just how to use it when they didn't get their way. Discussions with the parents went as expected. They claimed they had no idea where their little three-year-old heard those words, but it must have been at the church's daycare. Really, that was what they said. After several warnings to the parents, the child was not permitted to return. Shortly thereafter, the parent was bragging on social media that their three-year-old kid was kicked out of daycare for cussing out the teacher. They were proud of that fact. If you are a parent or guardian of children, you have a huge influence on the type of person your kids will be. I hope that your first five years were positive times to remember. I also hope someone in your life took the time to tell you about Jesus or took you to Sunday School rather than educate you on how to spew foul language.

School Years

What I will call *phase two* is all about those early school years. I would like for you to think back as far as you can to see if you remember your first day in school. What was it like? Mine was a little scary. I had several *firsts* on that day. It started with a long ride on a school bus. I remember Mom taking me down the driveway to meet the bus. Those huge double doors opened up. There sat a HUGE guy, driving the bus. He was a farmer wearing a full pair of denim overalls. No doubt he had been wearing those same clothes on the farm that morning. I remember I could hardly step up on the first step, but I made it. Being the shy kid I was, I just jumped immediately into the first seat to avoid attention.

It was the first day I'd spent away from home or under the care of a very close family member. I felt like I was all alone. We attended a small school in a very small town. The school amassed all grades from first to seniors in high school. The halls were full of kids my size. There were also all sizes ranging up to near adults. All I wanted to do was get to my classroom as fast as I could. It was the first time I got to use my new lunch box. Inside was a PB&J and matching thermos with my drink. I wish I still had that Yellow Submarine lunchbox today; it would be worth a bundle.

Principals and teachers ran the schools on very strict discipline back years ago, and if you got in trouble at school, you might as well expect the teacher to call your parents. Boy, were there consequences when you got home.

Those younger folks will not appreciate these next remarks, and you might think our teachers back then were too hard on us, but I am proof that their methods worked just fine. I have a master's degree in engineering and a master's degree in business. I spent lots of time standing in the corner, standing in the hall, or standing at the chalkboard with my nose in a circle. Why? Because I quickly outgrew my shyness and became quite mischievous. I blame it on the influence of all my new buddies. This was the first sign that I was adapting to my own personality and that my surroundings imparted an influence. It was fun to be mischievous – until I got caught.

Those of you who have kids today can thank me, in part, if you do not have those old, tall gray pipe monkey bars at your school playground or a big merry-go-round with old, splintery wooden planks. Why should you thank me? Because I got hurt on those two pieces of playground equipment so many times that I had to be on the top of the school nurse's injury list. They never told us kids why they took them out. But, I knew.

There is one story I have to tell that relates directly to how others can influence us to do things we shouldn't. Even at an early age, our playground also had a very large swing set. There were four swings on each of the two sections. Each swing had chains approximately fifteen feet long, so we could really swing high. Being the boys we were, we just had to have a "Who can swing the highest?" competition. My buddies and I then decided not only was it fun to swing high but to see how high we could swing and then jump out of the seat. Needless to say, I didn't win, but I can tell you that blacktop and gravel are not the best landing surfaces for skin.

Take a few moments to think back to your early grade school days and see if you can remember how you began to grow as a person and who influenced you the most during those years. You began to shape your own life with that first taste of independence.

Junior High

Have you ever gone back and pulled out old pictures from when you were in junior high? If you have any, put this book down and go get them. If you are like me, it will give you a laugh (and likely anyone sitting around that sees those pictures as well). I am not sure why God created this phase of our lives because it is just about the most awkward period of life you could imagine. For most of us, junior high typically meant getting consolidated to a new school facility. That meant more new people to meet. The biggest impact to me was that we only got one recess in junior high. I thought that was just awful.

Junior High was the beginning of those really awkward years as a person. I was short, overweight, had lots of freckles, was flat-footed, and had crooked teeth and bad hair. About the only thing I had going for me was that I was pretty smart, especially in math and science. Go ahead and say it, I was sort of a nerd. Stop laughing and go look at YOUR junior high picture!

Do you remember your first real boyfriend or girlfriend? Go back and look at their junior-high class picture while you have them out (I bet you did this anyway). This was probably the first time you really started noticing the opposite sex. For us boys, it was very easy for my parents to tell that I was "sweet on someone" because I actually started trying to comb my crazy farm boy hair, and I would try to sneak some of dad's after-shave (do you remember Hi-Karate?). I know Mom could smell it as I tried to run by her to catch the bus. Yes, sometimes, I used a little too much. I cannot speak for you ladies, but when a twelve-year-old boy starts worrying about his appearance, there has to be a girl involved somewhere.

You probably also met your first bully during these years. You may have even been one of those people that everyone made fun of and if you were like me, you were not part of the "popular kid crowd." You may have been a star athlete and everyone wanted to be like you. This might have even been the first time you even thought about what you wanted to do in life. I am sure you can still remember those adults who made an impact on your life during these couple of years.

Another change was responsibility. You, most likely, didn't notice that more accountability was being put on your shoulders. You most likely had to transfer buses to get to a new facility. You had to go to different classrooms and make sure you brought the right books and materials to each class. Your teachers probably had you start working on projects in class as part of a team. You had to start doing research for your school work and assignments. Your grades really started to mean something. They were preparing you for a big leap to high school.

Did you attend church while you were in junior high? If so, did you really want to go? Not me. Sunday night was when the Wonderful World of Disney was on. VCRs and DVRs didn't exist back then, so if you missed a show, you just missed it. To me, church was boring, but at least I got to sit with some of my buddies as long as we were quiet in service. This might have been the first time your parents let you sit in another pew with your friends.

If you did attend church, did you ever get into trouble for misbehaving? There was one particular Sunday morning service that I will always remember. Even to this day, I still laugh about what happened. My grandpa was the minister in our small Baptist church. He always ended the Sunday service by letting someone lead the closing prayer. Our church had this one guy who would pray... *forever*... when it was his turn. He was a really good guy, but he prayed for everything from world hunger to world peace to close the service. That one morning, my grandpa picked him to pray. All my buddies and I were sitting together, and we knew what was coming—at least five minutes of standing still in complete silence. Really, you expect four twelve-year-old boys to stand quietly for five-plus minutes? That day, it just didn't happen. About three minutes into this prayer, one of my friends' stomach growled so loud, everyone in the church heard it. That was all it took. Have you ever tried so hard not to laugh that it hurt? Needless to say, we didn't succeed. We all just cracked up. You know what, that guy just kept right on praying. We should have asked him to pray for all of our safety during the journey home because punishment was coming (and it did). I learned a lot about life in these junior high years as there began to be much more external influence on my life.

High School

Becoming a freshman is sort of a rite of passage for every kid. It is the next step in a kid's path, heading into adulthood and the real world. Once again, those four years began most likely with another change in their school's location, which was much larger than the junior high school.

This may have been the first time you as a teenager actually got to chose some of the classes you wanted like industrial arts. You were assigned a guidance counselor and maybe even a career counselor to help you to think about future plans out in the real world. Going to high school is a big step for everyone. This is where we all face the next level of responsibility as well as the first taste of what it means to become our own person with some new freedoms.

For most of us, one of the most memorable moments during high school years is getting a driver's license. Up to this point in your life, there is no other card or document that gives you the amount of responsibility and freedom as a driver's license can.

If you're like me, most of you remember your first car. I remember the kids from wealthier families who got new, cool cars to drive, but that wasn't my experience. My first taste of driving was either a beat up, old red Ford farm truck, or the brown family car, a Gran Torino. Do they even make brown cars these days? Only UPS trucks should be brown, in my opinion.

With a car comes *freedom*. Most of you can relate to that level of freedom, and I am sure you can remember your very first solo drive in a car without your parents. I remember pulling out of our driveway to go on my first solo drive. I pulled out nice and slow and drove very carefully – well, until I was out of my parents' sight. Then, I stepped on the gas.

Now I understand why insurance companies had higher insurance rates for teenage boys. I don't know if a car was as much of a rite of passage for girls as it was for boys, but that was my first real taste of being on my own. I ran around on Saturday nights with a guy who owned a 1972 Pinto (yes, the type that blew up). I don't know how that car ever remained roadworthy, but we certainly had our share of fun in it. Near the end of our high school years, we would decide what color we would spray paint the Pinto for the weekend. It was fun for everyone to guess what the next color would be. It was typically whatever my buddy could find in spray cans at the local store... on sale. The last color that the car wore before my buddy totaled it was gold. That was a fitting color for the end of that car's life.

Sometime during these four years, you will most likely experience your first date. You remember a few pages ago, reading that description of myself? That didn't change much until late in my senior year, so I am not giving any details about my first date other than to say *it did not go well*. I was shy, awkward, not an athlete, and definitely not a guy who would easily catch a girls' attention. That period was not a fun time for me. So, I focused most of my efforts into my classes, but more than any-thing, my time was spent just having fun with several buddies on the weekends.

As the calendar began to roll, seemingly swiftly, toward my grad-uation, I really had not spent much time even thinking about a career or what I might do once I graduated. Because I more or less goofed off in high school, I was one of those A/B students. I took some harder classes, but I was not a straight-A student who took more advanced classes and was solely focused on getting scholarships for college. My family was poor, so I never figured college was an option for me. Thank the good Lord that He sent someone my way before graduation, and that person asked me a simple question for which I didn't have an answer. He simply asked, "What will you do the day after graduation?" That person was my grandpa.

I had always held my grandpa in high esteem. I respected him more than anyone else in my life. He had lived through the Great Depression and was extremely poor as most people were. He worked hard and made a huge success of his life, but most importantly, he was a very dedicated Baptist minister. He made a difference in the lives of every person he met.

You always knew where my grandfather had been because he left a lapel pin of small, praying hands with every person he met. I admired that. When he asked that question, it made me realize it was time for a career decision. Because of his help and influence, I signed up for engineering school. If you think God does not work in your life, my story of getting into college is nothing short of a miracle. God puts us where He wants us – even if we may not be following Him as close as we should.

My college years were the time I really learned to trust God, and boy did He surround me with just the right Christian friends that I needed. My high school friends were not the right kind of influence. God knew that. With average grades, no physics classes, no SAT score, and only basic math classes, my grandpa took me to meet with the dean of the School of Engineering personally. After an hour of discussion, the dean looked at me and said, "If I let you in this school, will you finish?" The only answer that I had was "Yes." On top of getting into engineering school, it was a private school and very expensive. Remember, my family was poor, but that never became an issue. God made a way for me to work and go to school because he knew that was where I needed be. God already had people lined up to influence my life... *and did they ever.*

If you think God does not put people in your path to get your attention, I have breaking news. Yes, He does. As I said, it was a miracle that I even got into college, but more than that, God's plan for my life started the day I moved to campus. I was assigned a guest room in the dormitory because there were too many students enrolled for the first semester, and the university was short of housing. I had no idea who my roommate was; I just knew he was not from my area. His parents and mine amazingly arrived at the same time on a Saturday, and so, we just helped each other move in. It was a pretty good start. Then, the parents left. This was the first time I was really *completely* on my own. The first word that came to my mind was *FREEDOM!* Sunday morning came and all I could think about was sleeping in and being lazy. No early morning farm chores and, for the first time, I didn't have to go to church. It was about 8:00 am and my new roommate's alarm went off like a blaring symphony.

He got up and asked, "Why aren't you going to church?"

I couldn't believe it. I was 200 miles away from home, no parents, no intent to go to church, but God had other plans. It didn't take long for me to meet an outstanding group of friends who all just happened to be Christians. Needless to say, these four years were where I learned to get close to God. Who would have ever thought a poor farm boy from the middle of nowhere could get through an expensive private engineering school with almost no credentials and no advance planning? I learned that God was in control. I have learned that's just how God works. It wasn't all easy, but God got me through it. He also provided a great job near my home. When I went off to college, I originally had no intention of ever going back to my home town. I wanted to get as far away as I could, but God had other plans.

It is this time of life when you have had to decide between going to college, heading straight into the workforce, joining the military, or living in mom and dad's basement, playing video games. Do you see how much more responsibility is being placed on you to make decisions about your own life? Please take a moment and think back during this time of your life to remember those important people who really helped shape your life, along with anyone who helped you along with these difficult decisions. Those people helped you make critical decisions that would impact the rest of your life.

Adulthood

Finally, you have come to the point in your life when you consider yourself an adult. Some of you might have extended that carefree life if you went to college on mom and dad's payment plan. If you were like me, I had to take out loans and work part-time to pay for college. Not passing a class was not an option for me since I was paying for school. Bottom line, it was time to grow up.

It wasn't long before most of you found that special someone that just made your heart skip a beat (in a good way). Remember your proposal? I proposed to my wife in a really beautiful park. It was late in the evening, there was a slight drizzle, there were cute ducks on the pond, and we were standing on a little bridge. That was where I popped the question. Little did my wife know that park was on the grounds of the State Mental Hospital. She didn't know it until I told her, so I knew she would always remember it. You chose each other then, sometime later you found yourself standing in front of a minister and a big crowd of people, making a lifelong promise to do everything in your power to protect, provide, and keep your family together. What a huge responsibility.

Then came children. If you don't have children, this part might be a little foreign for you, but you might get a few laughs, anyway. Kids will change your life. I don't care how many books you read, kids will consume your time because that is really what they want most. They prefer your time and attention more than all the cool toys or video games you can buy them.

The night before my wife and son came home from the hospital, I was all alone in our house. A feeling of huge responsibility came over me like a tidal wave. For the first time, I realized I was responsible not only for my wife, but now also a new child. I was excited, but nervous too. What if I wasn't a good dad? What if I made mistakes with my son? The "what ifs" started rolling through my mind. This little voice from God reaffirmed me that it would be okay and that I was not the first dad in the world.

How many pictures and videos did you take of your first kid? Did you notice that you took way less photos if you had more than one child? The first child was your test case. You watched over, protected, guarded, and were ever so careful with that first one. You watched them grow quickly. You watched them as an infant sleeping in their little beds, hoping they didn't wake up so you could actually get some sleep. Have you noticed how adults forget the English language when they are around an infant? If those kids could talk back, they would be making fun of all the crazy sounds and words we make up. They just smile back and love us anyway. Do you remember the first diaper change? Boy, I do. Having shoveled lots of cow and pig manure, those did not even come close to changing a diaper! My son just looked up, smiled at me, and loved me anyway. Then came the first sounds and first words. If you were like me, I was so excited to hear "Da da." After a few months, I was looking for duct tape!

Toddler mobility was next on the list. We so encouraged our kids to walk, then just like talking, we wished they would slow down. T-ball, soccer, football, and many activities started filling our lives and, before we knew it, that little baby we brought home from the hospital was ready to start their own life. All too quickly, I watched my own son go through these first phases of life. I was optimistic because his mother and I had always instilled in him that God had to be in his life. No matter how difficult things got, God was in control.

Do you remember when your first kid got their driver's license? Do you remember their first date? Do you remember the first

15

time they went through a breakup? Were you involved in their life decisions? Among all of the activities of life, did you teach them about God? Did you go with them to church? Did you show them how important God was in their life?

The time finally came for you to watch this same cycle of life phases happen with your own children. The level of responsibility and stress is likely the highest at this point in your life. You have progressed from dependency on others to having others depend on you.

Welcome to the real world.

Dependency on Others

I honestly hope each of you that read this book have had a few laughs at yourself and me as you thought back through your life. I briefly took you back through your own life to get you to remember that there have been a lot of people that have had input in your life. You did not *do life* on your own. That input was high at the beginning, faded during the middle, and then will return late in your life. Regardless of your age, I am sure you will agree with me that life is very short. We spend these few years we have preparing for the final phase.

After you have read through these brief phases of life, you should be noticing a pattern. We learn things really fast, but also have a significant amount of help and influence from others that shape who you are. The amount you depend on others declines in direct proportion to your learning. Bottom line, we become independent very quickly and then return to that state of dependency near the end of life.

Our modern society and medical advances have extended our lifespan. At the writing of this book, a very recent study indicates the average lifespan is approximately eighty years for both women and men. Regardless of how long you live, we eventually all come to the final phase of life where we must face the fact that we will not live forever here on earth. That brings us to the real focus of this book and back to the title.

The title of this book drives you to a very similar question my grandpa asked me before I graduated from high school. That question is, where will you be the day after you die?

The Final Phase of Physical Life

There are times in life when it seems almost mandatory that we attend events that just do not register very high on our fun meter. I cannot speak for the ladies, but for guys, there are times we just don't want to be in public. We are busy, our attention span is short, we get hungry, we want to be watching sports, and we get bored really fast. If an activity is not on fire or moving over 100 miles per hour, it likely does not have our attention. These events to which I am referring are what I like to call "life events." When guys attend these life events, our minds are typically thinking about some project that needs a repair, who is ahead in the ball game, where we could be fishing, or we hear the golf course calling. We want to be anywhere other than at this event. The longer we live, the more of these life events we attend. I am now old enough that I can look back with some experience and wisdom that just might help younger readers of this book when it comes to these types of events.

As a senior citizen, (I guess that is me because I am retired, and I keep getting AARP cards in the mail) I have created a shortlist of the life events that are just not at the top of the fun list: family reunions especially when you have never met most of the family from some far-away state; high school reunions when you know someone who, after thirty-five years still colors their hair, gets a spray tan, or has to show up in a limo; graduations of kids when you barely know their parents, but you get that expected "send me a gift card" and sit through hearing 400 other names being read because your invitee has a last name that starts with a "Z." There are also events such as the ever-dreaded dance recital or elementary school band concert where earplugs are recommended. This list could go on, but you get the point. As I go over my experiences, there is one event that tops my list of "I really don't want to go." That is a funeral. You might think that statement is a little irreverent, but how many people like to go to funerals? The older you get, the more funerals you will attend.

As I stated earlier, my age is now past the standard highway speed limit (not the speed limit in Kentucky), and I find that I am attending an ever-increasing number of funerals for friends and family. I have noticed that in recent years, many funeral homes have caught onto the idea of making this last event for a person a celebration of life by running a video with pictures of the deceased, showing the years of their lives. I remember the old show, "This is Your Life." That is what I think of as I watch photos of someone's life flash by on a TV screen. With iPhones everywhere and my family always wanting to take pictures, I am trying to be more selective of every picture taken now. I know my family quite well and those goofy or embarrassing pictures will show up at my funeral. If you are like me, I really do not like going to the funeral home and, even more so, when the deceased is a relative, friend, or loved one that was close to me who's made an impact on my life. Those times seem to be even more stressful when the passing of that loved one is sudden or unexpected. The more of these funerals I attend, I discovered something. I've begun to watch these videos with intent as they tell you a lot about the person who passed. In addition to watching these life-in-review videos, I have also become more intentional about listening to the conversations during the visitation times and the message of the speaker at the service. You can learn a lot about a person while standing in a funeral visitation line if you just listen.

This interest in eavesdropping in the funeral lines became ever so clear to me at the recent funeral of a family member who had been tragically killed in an accident. While standing in the waiting line, I once again heard similar words that I have heard so many times at previous funerals. Being an engineer, I began to make mental notes and I find some some common themes from the words I heard. See if you have heard remarks like these at a funeral:

- They were a really good person.
- There is peace in knowing that they are now in a better place.
- People have only good things to say about them.
- They were a great person and would do anything for anyone because that is just who they were.
- I am so happy because they left a good legacy.
- Everybody loved them.

As I heard these words, my mind immediately thought about this person's legacy. The comments were all about this person being *good*. I have noticed you will rarely, if ever, hear anything bad in a funeral line about the person who passed away. Everything you hear is almost always positive. Regardless of how that person lived, everyone wants this person to be remembered as a "good person." This need to want everyone to be *considered good* is the heart of the message I hope to cover in this book. It strikes me as sad that many of us wait until a tragic moment or when we know the end of life is very near that we really give serious thought to the final phase of our existence. I need to ask you at this point, does being good have anything to do with where you will be the day after you die?

God's Spirit led me to the thought, "I wonder what words will be said in my viewing line?" What legacy will I leave? Will it be one where people say "He was a good man," or will they say, "He was a man that loved God and served him with all of his heart"? Each one of us will leave a legacy or impression on those remaining here. What words do you want people to say in your viewing line?

In 2014, I was asked to give a portion of my grandfather's eulogy. Even though there was no doubt in my mind that my grandfather was in Heaven, and I loved him very much, the task was still very difficult. My grandfather was a Baptist minister for the majority of his life, and he was a huge influence on me, my career, and my professional life. More than that, he was an influence that ensured I knew the foundations of the Christian faith, most importantly, the Gospel of Jesus Christ. My grandfather never met a stranger, and he prayed for every person who had those praying hands. He was also one of the most giving individuals I ever knew. I don't know how he did it, but he gave away more than I thought he could ever earn on a civilian's government salary. He was living proof of the scripture "give and it shall be given unto you."

As I prepared my short portion of his eulogy, I wondered what people were saying about him in his waiting line. I thought about the legacy he left and how I considered him much more than a good man. I wanted to ensure people really knew who my grandfather was and what impact his life had on those around him. I knew without a doubt that the final phase of his existence was being spent in Heaven. He had given his life to serving Jesus Christ. I knew where he was spending his eternity because he was *more* than a good person.

Shortly after the passing of my grandfather, I was blessed to be able to retire from my professional career, working as an engineer. I am very cautious about claiming "God told me to do something," because I have seen way too much of that in our religious communities today. Therefore, my next statement is made with caution. I felt the Holy Spirit began to minister to me that God had more work He wanted me to do that had nothing to do with being an engineer. The words in the title of this book just kept going through my mind over and over again. It came to the point that my mind would be thinking – almost continually – about being a good person and how many people in our society feel that just being a *good* person will gain you access into God's heavenly kingdom. I wrestled with this leading of the Holy Spirit, wondering what God wanted me to do with these few words. Like most people, I sort of ignored that leading, thinking maybe it was just the moment or an emotional feeling. Then, one afternoon at the funeral of another family member who'd passed away very unexpectedly, I literally heard these same words come from a relative of the deceased. It was clear God was wanting my attention devoted to this topic.

I don't want to get theological on you here, but I must ask, do you ever think about the fact that we humans are very different than any other creature on earth? If we are so very different, then there must be more to our existence. Doesn't that make you wonder why we are here, and what happens to us after we live our last day on this earth? We will all come to that day at some point in the future. How are you going to approach that day? We are about to get into the heart of this book, and I hope you hang in here through this discussion about how you are fearfully and wonderfully made.

As a Sunday school teacher for over thirty years, I have always wanted to ensure those attending my classes were fully aware that we are eternal beings created in the image of God. Having studied several sciences, the laws of thermodynamics are pretty convincing that we did not evolve from monkeys. You might be one of those scientific types that will argue, so here is a deal for you. You come up with something that violates the second law of thermodynamics and you come see me. I will work with you to obtain a patent, and we will be very rich.

In addition to this teaching that God created us in His image, I have stressed that God's Word is very clear on what His expectations are for us to enter His holy kingdom. Those requirements and expectations are clearly written in His Word and very simple to understand.

Yet, when I listen to people talk during funerals, it is clear they are unaware of the life after this one and the fact that it is real. My intent with this book is not to offend anyone in any way, I am just following the guidance of God's Holy Spirit to provide a wake-up call to our current approach to life and how little emphasis we place on where we will spend eternity. Many today think all they have to do is be a "good" person, and God will just whisk them right through the pearly gates to a better place. Based on the Bible, I am sure that is not the way it works. While as humans confined to these earthly bodies, we will never understand the mechanics of how we move from temporal beings into the eternal beings that God created, but God's Word gives us much insight into how we successfully make that transition.

I am quite confident many people do not have a clear understanding of their destiny after this life or what happens when we pass away – because we do not want to think or talk about death, or the final phase of our existence. Our destiny is determined by the choices we make while here on earth. The most frequent comment I hear about a person that has passed away is, "Well, they are in a better place." There are multiple books from every religion already written that discuss the topic of what happens to us after this life on earth ends. Generally speaking, research has shown that no matter where you travel on this planet, people from all walks of life believe in a higher creator or god of some kind. Where did that knowledge come from? Being a person of the Christian faith, I have a keen awareness that God created us to be eternal beings. God has given each individual a free choice to accept His requirements to spend eternity with Him or completely separated from Him. Most people ignore the eternal segment of their existence. That is what this book is about. The choices we each make during our life will determine our eternal residence in one of two places.

If you believe there is an existence after this physical life on earth, you need to consider what that existence is. If you are like nearly 85% of the humans that live on earth today, you likely believe there is a God or a great creator who decides where your eternal existence will be when you die. Coincident with this basic belief that there is a God, many have a feeling that our life after this one is somehow dependent on how we lived while we are physically alive. Many people today have their own interpretation of God and much of that interpretation is based on what they have heard or how they were raised, but mostly, their interpretation is one that justifies their lifestyle. Many today convince themselves they are living *good enough* to warrant a good existence after this physical life.

The purpose of the following chapters is to assemble the evidence that there is an eternal existence each one of us will experience – in one of two places – and there are very clearly defined paths that get you to these two destinations spelled out in God's Word. This journey starts with a question... Who defines what is good?

Other Questions for you to Consider

- Who influenced your life and who is in control of your life today?
- Was there a time in your life where you felt God's influence?
- Do you consider yourself a "good person?"

Chapter 2

Who defines What is Good?

Would you consider yourself a good person? Most people will say *yes*. If you are one of those who said *yes*, I would ask you to take a few minutes, get out a piece of paper, and write down what you think makes you a good person. Before we talk in-depth about the true definition of a good person, we need to understand that, as humans, we have created our own individual labels of good and bad. It is through this individual lens we behave and view the world. This view shapes our beliefs and our attitude toward the eternal part of our existence when we pass away. Some do not think about existence after earth until they feel they are about to depart this life.

The word *good* is defined as: morally excellent; virtuous and righteous (The Random House College Dictionary First Edition 1975)

Our personal definition of *good* is tainted by our own prejudices and experiences. The critical point to be made here is that we are not the ones to define what (or who) is good; only the creator of the universe has that authority. What does He say about the definition of good? Let's look into His Word and see.

> *He that is without sin among you, let him first cast*
> *a stone at her. (John 8:7 KJV)*

One of my favorite scriptures in the Bible is found in John 8:2-11. This is the record of the adulterous woman the religious leaders brought to Jesus. It always amazed me that they forgot to bring the man who was just as guilty as the woman. The heart of this scripture is when Jesus made the statement, "He that is without sin among you, let him first cast a stone at her." Every time I read this story, it opens my eyes to realize how many times in my life I have been just like those religious leaders standing there with a rock in my hand, passing judgment on anyone who does not meet my standard of moral living.

If you have read this story in the Bible, you will find that the religious leaders were always trying to tempt Jesus or trick Him into doing or saying something so they could find fault. These few verses tell us that Jesus knelt down and wrote in the dirt with His finger. I always wondered what Jesus wrote on the ground during this event. You can search the Internet and find many speculations about what He wrote, but we will never really know. The main point of this story, for me, is the fact no one is free of sin, no matter if you are a religious person who attends church every Sunday or you're a vile criminal. We are all guilty. I will admit upfront, I am not a perfect person, in fact, very far from it. God reminds us in Romans 3:23 that all have sinned and come short of the glory of God. I am at the top of the list. I needed (and still need) His forgiveness every day of my life. Just like those religious leaders surrounding Jesus and that woman, our own conscience will condemn us.

Jesus clearly knew the Mosaic Law and the sin of adultery was punishable by death through stoning. The most important part of this story to me is that Jesus did not condemn this woman even though she was caught in the very act of what society considered a *bad* sin. Jesus finished His statement by telling the woman, "Go and sin no more." This is where we struggle today because we do not want to stop our selfish and sinful behavior, yet we want to judge others based upon our personal definition of being a good person. Have you ever found yourself justifying your actions even if they might have been questionable?

While growing up, I never abused drugs, never drank alcohol, and I never smoked (except one puff on my dad's pipe, which made me turn green). I always obeyed my parents, although I griped a lot. I was never arrested or had problems with law enforcement. My life has been pretty clean, except for a single speeding ticket. I made fairly good grades in school, I was always home before my curfew, and I always went to church. Everyone described me as a "good kid." That list may sound similar to many of you reading this book. If you were like me, I was always taken to church and taught what was right and wrong. In my mind, I thought I was a pretty good person because I was comparing myself to all the kids around me that were getting into lots of trouble. I felt as long as I behaved better than them, I was okay. I knew deep inside that was not the case and that something was clearly missing. That thought process is like being in the forest when a bear is chasing you and another person. You just have to be faster than the other person to avoid the bear. When it comes to disobedience to God, it will always catch up to you.

Even after becoming a Christian early in my life, I often found myself passing judgment on those that lived "in sin" and were not good like me. I looked at those that were into drugs, alcohol, premarital sex, cheating on their spouse, living together outside of marriage, telling lies, using foul language, never kind to anyone, and generally having a bad attitude as those who were not as good as me. My definition of *good* was all about attending church, not using foul language, avoiding drugs and narcotics, and generally just staying out of trouble. It took a long time for me to realize these behaviors are *not* what it means to be *good* in God's eyes.

While on a short family vacation, one Sunday morning at the age of ten, while in a church in Bowling Green, Kentucky, a Sunday School teacher was telling us about why Jesus died for our sins. There was no vision of heaven, no bright light, no angel messenger; I heard no thunder and saw no lightning. I just heard a small voice that said I needed to follow Jesus. I heard that voice in my mind and it simply told me, *I needed to listen to Jesus and ask Him to forgive me of my sins.* I really felt this calling, so I said, "Sure, why not?" When we returned home from our short vacation, my grandfather (the Baptist minister) sat me down and asked me a whole bunch of questions to make sure I really knew what choice I was making. He agreed that Jesus was calling me, and I was later baptized in a local creek. Boy, was my grandfather happy. I was now saved!

This sounds like a wonderful story, but here comes the real part. Even though I had made that decision to follow Jesus at ten years of age and continued to go to church, I strayed from the life I knew I should have been living. As I grew through my teenage years, I became a very angry young person with a bad attitude and a mouth that often accompanies a bad attitude. But, I was still that "good boy" because all of the good things I listed above I kept doing. I was putting on a pretty good show for everyone and did I have them fooled. Compared to my buddies, I was *good*. I was really good at hiding my darker side.

I have no intention of debating the old "once saved, always saved" issue here, but I can tell you without a doubt had I died during my teenage years, I do not believe I would have been allowed into God's eternal kingdom even though I made that commitment to serve Jesus when I was ten. I knew most of the church hymnal songs, I could quote some scriptures, and I could say a religious prayer with the best of those in church, but I was not keeping God's commandments, and I did not have a real love for Him. I was doing these things to *look* the part and those were just things you were supposed to do if you called yourself a Christian. I was going through the motions of living a "religious" life, but there was no personal relationship with Jesus inside my life. I was living out the verse of scripture in Matthew 15:8 where Jesus said, "This people draweth nigh unto me with their mouth, and honoureth me with their lips; but their heart is far from me." I thought I was good because I didn't break the big sins. I was just like those religious leaders Jesus called out with the adulterous woman. I am guilty of sin.

Little Sins and Big Sins

As we exist today in our high-tech society, the word "good" has become a relative term. We determine that we are good as long as we are better than those around us. This mentality perme-ates the Christian faith because we have decided that there are "big sins" and "little sins." If you commit one of the little sins, that is okay and God just looks the other way. But if you commit one of those big ones, you are just a total heathen... especially if you get caught.

Let's put this definition of big sins and little sins to the test. If I kill someone, is that worse than if I lie to someone? If I steal a car, is that worse than telling a dirty joke? If I cheat on my spouse, is that worse than gossiping about my neighbor? You have to admit, there is something inside of us that says *murder is worse than telling a little lie.*

How do you think God views sin?

Our individual definition of "good" is all about the standard by which we use to measure. Man's standard is flawed; God's standard is perfect, fair, and true. We must understand, God sets the standard for the definition of "good," not us. That standard will be used at some point in the future to evaluate the lives we lived while in these physical bodies. God's word clearly says, in Hebrews 9:27, "And as it is appointed unto men once to die, but after this the judgment." God's Word also tells us in 2 Corinthians 5:10, "For we must all appear before the judgment seat of Christ; that every one may receive the things *done* in *his* body, according to that he hath done, whether *it be* good or bad." We will discuss these two scriptures later in this book. We will all stand before Jesus Christ and give an account of our lives. That life review will be compared to the only true definition of good that was defined by God Himself. Jesus will not say "you were better than Fred (or Susie), so I will let you into heaven. The actions of your life will be compared to the set of requirements God has established. The psalmist describes the general corrupt condition of natural man

> *The fool hath said in his heart, There is no God. They are corrupt, they have done abominable works, there is none that doeth good. The LORD looked down from heaven upon the children of men, to see if there were any that did understand, and seek God. They are all gone aside, they are all*

> *together become filthy: there is none that doeth*
> *good, no, not one.* (Psalms 14:1-3)

For us to understand the term *good* from God's perspective and learn about His standard, we must continue to go to His Word. It is pretty amazing that the first chapter in the first book of the Bible gives us God's definition of *good*. We find in that first chapter of the book of Genesis as God was creating the universe and all living creatures here on earth, there are several times where He said, "and it was good." Here they are for your reference:

> *And God said, Let there be light: and there was*
> *light. And God saw the light, that it was good:*
> *and God divided the light from the darkness.*
> (Genesis 1:3-4)

> *And God called the dry land Earth; and the*
> *gathering together of the waters called the Seas:*
> *and God saw that it was good.* (Genesis 1:10)

> *And the earth brought forth grass, and herb*
> *yielding seed after his kind, and the tree yielding*
> *fruit, whose seed was in itself, after his kind: and*
> *God saw that it was good.* (Genesis 1:12)

> *And to rule over the day and over the night, and*
> *to divide the light from the darkness: and God saw*
> *that it was good.* (Genesis 1:18)

> *And God created great whales, and every living*
> *creature that moveth, which the waters brought*
> *forth abundantly, after their kind, and every*

winged fowl after his kind: and God saw that it was good. (Genesis 1:21)

And God made the beast of the earth after his kind, and cattle after their kind, and every thing that creepeth upon the earth after his kind: and God saw that it was good. The problem science has with God.. There is no evidence, only faith. (Genesis 1:25)

And God saw every thing that he had made, and, behold, it was very good. And the evening and the morning were the sixth day. (Genesis 1:31)

God originally made everything in the universe *good*. In fact, I do not believe we fully understand what kind of person Adam was when God created him. God clearly said, "Let us make man in our image." This means that Adam was originally made to live forever. He was likely a genius on the IQ scale; he was extremely aware of God's existence and presence, and he loved God more than anything else on earth. Most important, God gave Adam that free will to choose to obey Him or not. Everything here on planet earth was *good* until mankind did one thing. They disobeyed God. The definition of good became different for Adam.

How does eating a piece of fruit from a tree in the middle of a garden rank on your list of big sins vs. little sins? A simple way to remember God's definition of good is living in obedience to His commands. Adam simply chose to disobey God's commandment. That is why Jesus told us in John 14:15, "If you love me, keep my commandments." If you are like me, after we have accepted Jesus Christ as our Savior (which is the first requirement to enter Heaven), we then have to work to obey

God despite all of the negative influences of this society. It does not take very long for us to depart from a path if we become distracted. An excellent example is distracted driving. Cell phones can easily pull your focus from the road; it only takes seconds for your car to veer over the line. It is the same with our spiritual lives. Our enemy is spending all of his energy trying to distract God's children from the righteous path into a path of disobedience.

You might ask yourself, "How can this happen if we are God's children?" Have you ever had a friend talk you into doing something you knew was wrong, but you went along with the plan just so you would fit in with the group? See how easily we can be distracted into making bad choices... even by our friends?

If you do the math of the lifespans of the people listed in Genesis chapter 5, you will find that within about 1550 years, mankind went from personally walking with God in the Garden of Eden to the point that every thought and imagination in man's heart became evil. Mankind let disobedience to God take over within our hearts, our minds, and our actions.

> And GOD saw that the wickedness of man was great in the earth, and that every imagination of the thoughts of his heart was only evil continually. (Genesis 6:5)

We are Basically Bad from the Beginning

Evil does not exist, or at least it does not exist unto itself. Evil is simply the absence of God. It is just like darkness and cold. Evil is a word that man has created to describe the absence of God. God did not create evil. Evil is the result of what happens when man does not have God's love present in his heart. It's like the cold that comes when there is no heat or the darkness that results when there is no light. It is the opposite of good. God has clearly defined what is good and what is bad in His Word. We are basically bad the moment we are born. Think about this, what do most kids do when they get caught doing something they know they are not supposed to do? They lie about what they did. It does not matter that they are standing with a crayon in their hand – one that matches the color of the marks on the wall. They will still lie. Did you teach them how to do that? I don't think most parents sit their kids down and say, "I am going to teach you how you tell a lie to get you out of trouble." It just comes naturally. That is why God says there is "none that doeth good", no, not one.

Growing up as a child with a mother who was a preacher's kid made life a little more difficult for me than for most of my early childhood friends. Not only were behavioral expectations very high for me, there were all those "words you can't say" that all the other boys could say, but not me. To this day, there is a word that brings shivers to my body when I hear it. As I stated earlier, we grew up on a farm, and on our farm, we did everything the hard way.

Hard work was an everyday occurrence for us. One day my sweet innocent (or so mom thought) little sister was not doing her job and I told her she needed to get her b??t in gear and help. The moment that word came from my mouth, my sister's eyes opened wide, her mouth dropped open, and off she ran to tattle on me. The reaction from my mom was just about what I expected. She called me into the house and proceeded to wash my mouth out with the nearest substance she could get her hands on in the bathroom that wasn't poisonous. It just happened to be my dad's can of Barbasol shaving cream. Where was Child Protective Services back in 1975? Needless to say, I didn't die from the experience, I was not traumatized for life, but that memory left a mark on me to this day. Even though that word is a very commonly used word today to describe a part of our anatomy and it is really not a "bad word," I still get a bad taste in my mouth every time I hear it. If you have not figured out the word yet, it is "butt." So, just to get back at my mom, that word is in this book for everyone to read. How is that for revenge after forty-five years? That word likely makes this a PG-13 rated book. So, sorry if that affects how you feel about this book.

You might ask yourself, where is this going, and what does that crazy story have to do with who defines *good*? Pretty simple, I lived in Mom's house, and Mom made the rules. So, in my early childhood, it was Mom who determined what was good and bad, not me. In addition, it was Mom who determined the consequences for breaking the rules. It didn't matter if I liked the rules that determined what was good or bad, I still had to live within those rules or face the consequences. It was pretty clear to me who made the rules for our home, Mom and Dad. It was their home and their rules.

Following this line of reasoning and the verses of scripture in Genesis, it is not difficult to figure out that we live in the universe that God created. Since this is His house, He makes the rules. Therefore, it is God alone that has the right to make the rules that determine what is right and wrong, and He has the right to determine the consequences for breaking His rules. It does not matter if we like the rules and consequences or not. God will not accept excuses for disobedience, and we cannot lie to cover our bad choices. As a direct result of our decision to break God's laws, we shouldn't be surprised at the resulting chaos and negative consequences, nor should we be surprised about the associated punishment that follows the breaking of His laws. We will talk about those consequences later in this book.

Our politically correct society is all about not offending anyone. We just want everyone to live as they desire even to the point of openly breaking God's laws as long as it feels good to them. If we tell someone they are not supposed to do something today, we have offended them, and now it is called "hate speech." Did you ever intentionally do something simply because someone else told you not to do it? That is where we are spiritually today. The theme of our society has become something like "how dare anyone (even God) tell me I can't do something, I want to do it, and I am going to do what I want." Herein lies the problem. Mankind has pushed God out of our lives, so the standard for defining *good* now resides in us and not God. By doing this, we have removed God and put mankind into the role of defining what is *good*. Given we are all flawed and sinful beings, we do not have the capability to properly define *good* and hold to that standard. We will allow our definition of good to fit the circumstances. Mankind has assumed the role of defining good and bad as well as any consequences that result from this mindset. How is this working for us today? Not so good. Samuel tells us that man's heart is the source of this conflict:

> But the LORD said unto Samuel, Look not on his countenance, or on the height of his stature; because I have refused him: for the LORD seeth not as man seeth; for man looketh on the outward appearance, but the LORD looketh on the heart. (1 Samuel 16:7)

After many years, I began to finally grow in my Christian faith. Going back to the story of the adulterous woman, I realized that I certainly cannot cast stones at anyone. Being a person needing the forgiveness of Jesus Christ in my life, I now try to see people in a different manner. I need to be forgiven for my sins just as much as anyone else. I must forgive others before God will forgive me. I am no better than those that I would label as bad. We must learn not to throw rocks at anyone. Several years of God's patience and a few life-changing decisions later, my story did a 180-degree turn. You will have to read Chapter 7 to see how God changed me from the inside out, but I finally started to learn that it is God that decides what is good. I learned that being good is much more than going to church, staying out of trouble, and being nice to people. Being *good*, according to God, is all about putting Him first in your life, obeying His commands and then letting Him make the changes that are needed. He changes us from the inside out. We will never be able to clean ourselves up on our own; we require His forgiveness.

In addition to the fact that we live in God's created universe, He also instilled within us a universal code of morality. Did you ever stop and think about the fact that no matter where you go on earth, people have the same general knowledge of what is right and wrong? Regardless of a person's ethnicity, culture, race, or religion (or lack of), there are basic actions that are just wrong. Examples are murder, lying, cheating, stealing, and abuse. All we have to do today is watch the news, and we can see the direct results of breaking these laws by the negative impact on society. Violating this internal moral code leads to a society full of chaos because mankind has now taken the role of defining *good*.

Breaking God's single, simple rule (eating the fruit from the tree) resulted in a consequence of immediate ejection from the Garden of Eden and a future death. It resulted in the separation from God's direct, daily contact with mankind. It ultimately ended with the curse of death for all of us. If you read the Bible at all, you will find for yourself that it did not take very long for society to deteriorate. It all started with disobedience of a single, simple command. This concept of being good should now be pretty simple to understand, as well as the consequences that follow. When we willingly disobey God's commands, we separate ourselves from Him. If you are a person that may not have gone to church and you may have never really read the Bible, you might claim that you don't know God's rules. I have no intension of influencing you; I will simply print here the words of Jesus Himself and what He says about obedience to God:

> *Master, which is the great commandment in the law? Jesus said unto him, Thou shalt love the Lord thy God with all thy heart, and with all thy soul, and with all thy mind. This is the first and great commandment. And the second is like unto it, Thou shalt love thy neighbour as thyself. On these two commandments hang all the law and the prophets.* (Matthew 22:36-40)

> *And when he was gone forth into the way, there came one running, and kneeled to him, and asked him, Good Master, what shall I do that I may inherit eternal life? And Jesus said unto him, Why callest thou me good? there is none good but one, that is, God. Thou knowest the commandments, Do not commit adultery, Do not kill, Do not steal, Do*

not bear false witness, Defraud not, Honour thy
father and mother. (Mark 10:17-19)

So, who defines what is good? The answer is: God does. Not
only does God set the rules, He wrote them in His Word and
He designed every human with those basic rules engraved into
our soul. We will have no excuse by claiming ignorance of God's
rules. How do we know that God really put those rules into
our souls?

> *For when the Gentiles, which have not the law, do*
> *by nature the things contained in the law, these,*
> *having not the law, are a law unto themselves:*
> *Which shew the work of the law written in their*
> *hearts, their conscience also bearing witness, and*
> *their thoughts the mean while accusing or else*
> *excusing one another.* (Romans 2:14-16 KJV)

> *For the invisible things of him from the creation*
> *of the world are clearly seen, being understood by*
> *the things that are made, even his eternal power*
> *and Godhead; so that they are without excuse,*
> (Romans 1:20)

Other Questions for you to Consider

- Do you judge people unfairly based on your definition
  of good or bad?
- Do you measure your level of goodness by comparing
  yourself to others?
- Are you putting on a front to fool those around you?

Chapter 3

Man Became a Living Soul

D o you know that someday, in the near future, you will get to meet Jesus personally? Every human that has ever lived has a scheduled appointment to meet Jesus. You might ask, how do I know you and I will meet Jesus? This fact is based on the evidence written in God's word that He created us as an eternal being, and once this physical body dies, that eternal component has an appointment to keep with Jesus. That appointment will be when we stand in His presence for a review of the life we lived while here on earth. This is an appointment that we will not miss, in fact, we cannot even be late. Attendance to this appointment is mandatory, and we are not in control of the schedule.

> *For we must all appear before the judgment seat of Christ; that every one may receive the things done in his body, according to that he hath done, whether it be good or bad.*
> (2 Corinthians 5:10 KJV)

To understand this future appointment we each have approaching, we must first understand how God created us in the three different parts. We have to begin this discussion by going back into the book of Genesis and reading about the creation of mankind.

To understand how moral laws and God's definition of good were put into our soul, we must understand how God created us. The writer of the Book of Genesis summed up the human making process in just a few verses. We also have two more verses in the New Testament that describe our makeup that we will discuss here as well.

We are Created in Three Parts Just Like God

> *And God said, Let us make man in our image, after our likeness: and let them have dominion over the fish of the sea, and over the fowl of the air, and over the cattle, and over all the earth, and over every creeping thing that creepeth upon the earth. So God created man in his own image, in the image of God created he him; male and female created he them.* (Genesis 1:26-27 KJV)

> *And the LORD God formed man of the dust of the ground, and breathed into his nostrils the breath of life; and man became a living soul.* (Genesis 2:7 KJV)

> *And the very God of peace sanctify you wholly; and I pray God your whole spirit and soul and body be preserved blameless unto the coming of our Lord Jesus Christ.* (1 Thessalonians 5:23 KJV)

> *For the word of God is quick, and powerful, and sharper than any two edged sword, piercing even to the dividing asunder of soul and spirit, and of the joints and marrow, and is a discerner of the thoughts and intents of the heart.* (Hebrews 4:12 KJV)

From the verses in Genesis 1, we learn that humans were made after a pattern, and that pattern had more than one component. A basic study of God's Word will lead you to the fact that He is made up of three parts: Father, the Son, and the Holy Spirit. I like to think maybe God was talking to Himself in Genesis 1:26 when He said, "Let us." We should be able to conclude that a human being has three parts to follow that pattern. This is confirmed by the two verses from the New Testament stated above.

The verse in Genesis 2:7 also gives a clue that God made us in two steps: He first formed our physical body from the dirt, then He literally blew His breath into that body to insert our soul and spirit. This act of inserting His breath makes us different than all of creation, and it is what made us a sentient being for the purpose of fellowship with the Creator. There is an excellent reference you can use to see the three parts of a person in Clarence Larkin's book, "Dispensational Truth in the World." Each of the three parts has a unique yet critical function.

Our Body

Your body is the physical part of your existence. This is the part God molded from the dirt and the part that will return to dirt a few years after you die (see Gen. 3:19). This is the part that will now grow old and pass away at some point in your future no matter how hard we try to stay in shape or live healthily. This is the part of you that interfaces with the physical world using your five senses of sight, smell, taste, touch, and hearing. I look at our senses, much like filters through which the environment of the world must pass to get into your conscience. I grew up on a farm, and I remember having to milk our cow each day. The milk went from the cow right into an old metal bucket that was not very clean. Before we would drink the milk, we would pour the milk through a large fabric filter that would strain out all of the "big chunks" of dirt and "other things" that would fall into the bucket during a milking session. This was not a time for cheap filters. I remember seeing all of the junk those filters separated that would have went right into our body. That is what your senses can do for you, they can be used to separate the junk from the world from the good that goes into your conscience, or they can allow anything to just pass right through. You are the one that decides the quality of your filters.

What is the Difference Between the Soul and the Spirit?

This might be a confusing part of this discussion. You can go online and research "What is the difference between the soul and the spirit?" and you will get dozens of results that try to describe this difference. You will find these two words seem to be used interchangeably throughout the Old and New Testaments, but the scriptures above in, 1 Thessalonians and Hebrews, make it clear there is a difference.

The words "soul" and "spirit" are found throughout the Bible, each occurring numerous times. The Hebrew word translated "soul" means a breathing creature, one in which life is present, whether physical life or mental life. The Greek word in the New Testament is similar. In its most basic sense, the word "soul" means "life," either physical or eternal. Jesus asks what it profits a man to gain the whole world and lose his soul, referring to his eternal life (Matt. 16:26). Both Old and New Testaments reiterate that we are to love God completely, with the whole *soul*, which refers to everything that is in us that makes us alive (Deut. 6:4-5; Mark 12:30). Whenever the word, "soul" is used, it can refer to the whole person, whether physically alive or in the afterlife.

> *Then shall the dust return to the earth as it was:*
> *and the spirit shall return unto God who gave it.*
> (Ecclesiastes 12:7 KJV)

To keep this discussion simple, this is the eternal part of your existence that returns to God when life here on Earth ends. This part of you will live forever in one of two places, within Heaven with God or completely separated from Him in Hell. You make that choice on your own while you are here on earth of your own free will by giving your life to Jesus Christ or not.

The Greek word used for *soul* is psyche, which is what you could consider the first level of your conscience being. This part of you consists of your memory, your reasoning, your imaginations, memory, and your affections. This is the component of your being where good and evil collide and a choice is made between the two. Paul refers to it as the natural man in 1 Corinthians 2:14.

> *But the natural man receiveth not the things of*
> *the Spirit of God: for they are foolishness unto*
> *him: neither can he know them, because they are*
> *spiritually discerned.* (1 Corinthians 2:14 KJV).

45

The word *spirit* is used to denote something different in Scripture, although both the Hebrew and Greek words translated *spirit* also have the concept of breath or wind at their roots. We understand the difference by looking at the context of the verses that refer to the spirit of man. Unlike the soul, which is alive both physically and eternally, the spirit can be either alive, as in the case of believers, (1 Pet. 3:18), or dead as unbelievers are (Col. 2:13; Eph. 2:4-5). The spiritual part of believers in Jesus Christ is that which responds to the things that come from the Spirit of God, understanding and discerning them spiritually. The spiritually dead perceive the things of the Spirit to be foolishness, because, in his spiritually dead conditions, he does not have the ability to discern the things of the Spirit (1 Cor. 2:12-14). The spirit is that part of us that is enabled by God to know and worship Him, the part of humanity that connects with God, who Himself is Spirit (John 4:24).

While the two words are often used interchangeably, the primary distinction between soul and spirit in man is that the soul is the animate life, or the seat of the senses, desires, affections, and appetites. The spirit is that part of us that connects, or refuses to connect, to God. Our spirits relate to His Spirit, either accepting His promptings and conviction, thereby proving that we belong to Him (Rom. 8:16) or resisting Him and proving that we do not have spiritual life (Acts 7:51).

If the Holy Spirit is resident in your Spirit and you are allowing your body to violate God's Laws, there is a battle ongoing in your soul because good and evil cannot coexist in us. Either your body or your Spirit will win the battle, not both.

Or else he will hold to the one, and despise the other. Ye cannot serve God and mammon. (Matthew 6:24 KJV)

The Greek word used for *Spirit* is *pneuma* and it means rational soul. This is the eternal component of our being and the part of us that connects, or refuses to connect, to God.

The spirit is the element in humanity that gives us the ability to have an intimate relationship with God. Whenever the word spirit is used, it refers to the immaterial part of humanity that connects with God, who Himself is spirit. (John 4:24)

We are Beings of Light

If you are a Star Wars fan, I am not going to go all Yoda on you here and talk about the force that binds the universe together. The Bible is pretty clear that the eternal part of our being has unique characteristics and, in many cases, refers to these characteristics as *light* because I think our human brains can at least understand this concept since we can see light.

Light is defined as: something that makes things visible or affords illumination. Darkness is defined as: the absence of light (The Random House College Dictionary, First Edition 1975)

When you read these definitions, can you see the spiritual implication these words have? How do these definitions relate to how we, as humans, are created? To continue this discussion about how we are created, we will dig a little deeper by going into the Bible to read several scriptures recorded in the Gospels that are associated with our spirit. The scriptures pertaining to our eternal existence are associated with the term *light*. Before

47

we discuss the light that is within us, we must first understand that it is God that "owns" this eternal part of our existence, as stated in the Old Testament.

> *Then shall the dust return to the earth as it was:*
> *and the spirit shall return unto God who gave it.*
> (Ecclesiastes 12:7)

Paul also says nearly the same thing in the New Testament.

> *What? know ye not that your body is the temple*
> *of the Holy Ghost which is in you, which ye have*
> *of God, and ye are not your own? For ye are*
> *bought with a price: therefore glorify God in*
> *your body, and in your spirit, which are God's.*
> (1 Corinthians 6:19-20)

We are now talking about the eternal part of our being that belongs to God and it is also referred to as light. The most informative scriptures about spiritual light relative to how we are created are found in the book of John and are included here for your reading:

> *In the beginning was the Word, and the Word was*
> *with God, and the Word was God. The same was*
> *in the beginning with God. All things were made*
> *by him; and without him was not any thing made*
> *that was made. In him was life; and the life was*
> *the light of men. And the light shineth in darkness;*
> *and the darkness comprehended it not. There was*
> *a man sent from God, whose name was John. The*
> *same came for a witness, to bear witness of the*
> *Light, that all men through him might believe. He*

was not that Light, but was sent to bear witness of that Light. That was the true Light, which lighteth every man that cometh into the world. (John 1:1-9)

He that believeth on him is not condemned: but he that believeth not is condemned already, because he hath not believed in the name of the only begotten Son of God. And this is the condemnation, that light is come into the world, and men loved darkness rather than light, because their deeds were evil. For every one that doeth evil hateth the light, neither cometh to the light, lest his deeds should be reproved. But he that doeth truth cometh to the light, that his deeds may be made manifest, that they are wrought in God. (John 3:18-21)

Jesus makes several references to light and darkness and I want to pull out a few of them just for your ease of reference:

Ye are the light of the world. A city that is set on an hill cannot be hid. Neither do men light a candle, and put it under a bushel, but on a candlestick; and it giveth light unto all that are in the house. Let your light so shine before men, that they may see your good works, and glorify your Father which is in heaven. (Matthew 5:14-16)

To give light to them that sit in darkness and in the shadow of death, to guide our feet into the way of peace. (Luke 1:79)

For mine eyes (Simeon) have seen thy salvation, Which thou hast prepared before the face of all people; A light to lighten the Gentiles, and the glory of thy people Israel. (Luke 2:30-32)

A short passage from Jesus in Luke gives us more detail about how we are created related to us being spiritual lights:

No man, when he hath lighted a candle, putteth it in a secret place, neither under a bushel, but on a candlestick, that they which come in may see the light. The light of the body is the eye: therefore when thine eye is single, thy whole body also is full of light; but when thine eye is evil, thy body also is full of darkness. Take heed therefore that the light which is in thee be not darkness. If thy whole body therefore be full of light, having no part dark, the whole shall be full of light, as when the bright shining of a candle doth give thee light. (Luke 11:33-36)

You might be asking yourself, "What does all of this discussion have to do with being good enough or not?" As eternal creatures, God calls us children of light. God's light through the Holy Spirit takes up residence inside of our spirit and we become a new creature from the inside out. The Holy Spirit can only move in when we accept Jesus Christ (who is defined as the light of life) as our personal Savior. This is the only way we can be good enough to enter God's kingdom, not by performing religious acts or just being a nice person. The eternal part of our existence must be filled with the spiritual light from God and that light must shine to all those around us. God clearly tells us, in the scriptures, I included above that sin separates us from God. When we chose to let sin exist and rule our lives, our spirit becomes dark (remember Webster's definition of dark is simply the absence of light). Darkness has no place in God's eternal kingdom. If your spirit is missing the light of Jesus Christ, you will not be *good* enough to enter God's Kingdom.

We were created to have the light of God within our spirit. In fact, His word tells us in, John 4:24, God is a Spirit: and they that worship him must worship him in spirit and in truth. We cannot worship God unless His light dwells within our spirit. That is also why when Jesus left this earth, He told His disciples that He "must go" away so that the Comforter can come. This comforter is the Holy Spirit that lights up the eternal part of our life. Without the Holy Spirit inside of you, you will be in the darkness of the world and subject to the evil temptations to violate God's laws.

The Light Makes Us Different

This may be difficult to accept, but when God's Spirit of light moves into our spirit, we become a new creature (2 Cor. 5:17), and the disobedient part of our lives should vanish. Just as light and darkness cannot coexist, Jesus was very clear that good and bad cannot come from someone within whom His Spirit lives.

> *Even so every good tree bringeth forth good fruit; but a corrupt tree bringeth forth evil fruit. A good tree cannot bring forth evil fruit, neither can a corrupt tree bring forth good fruit. Every tree that bringeth not forth good fruit is hewn down, and cast into the fire. Wherefore by their fruits ye shall know them.* (Matthew 7:17-20)

> *Out of the same mouth proceedeth blessing and*
> *cursing. My brethren, these things ought not so*
> *to be. Doth a fountain send forth at the same*
> *place sweet water and bitter? Can the fig tree, my*
> *brethren, bear olive berries? either a vine, figs? so*
> *can no fountain both yield salt water and fresh.*
> (James 3:10-12)

We have the free will to decide if we want His Spirit living in us or not. You make the choice to let His light in or you reject it. That light will bring clarity in a deceitful world that says we no longer have to keep God's laws. His light helps our living soul obey His rules.

I need to remind you that we ended the previous chapter with the scripture in Romans 1:20, that says we are "without excuse" and make the tie to this discussion about how we are created. I hope that you got a Bible and actually read the first three chapters of Genesis as that will make this association clear. You will now realize that excuses started with the very first sin? A quick read of the account of Adam and Eve eating the fruit from the tree ends with Adam blaming Eve for telling him to eat the fruit. Being a guy, how many times do us guys do what our wives tell us...really? Oh, by the way, if you read Adam's response in Genesis, you can even get the hint that Adam blamed God for giving him Eve in the first place! When God turned to Eve to ask what happened, what did she do? She blamed the serpent! You see, when we disobey God, we know we are in trouble, and no one needs to tell us our action was wrong. But, you will notice we start making excuses by blaming others or circumstances that caused us to disobey God. Our kids do not have to be taught to lie, they come by it naturally when they get caught breaking a rule. We start making excuses, which are just lies, from our earliest age. That philosophy began as soon as we disobeyed God and broke our internal moral code.

What are those rules we must obey so that our eternal being will reside in Heaven with God?

Other Questions for you to Consider

- Do you really understand there is an eternal part of you that will live forever?
- Have you considered where that part of you will exist after you die?
- Are you being a light to positively influence those around you?

Chapter 4

⛯

God has Rules

And the LORD God commanded the man, saying, Of every tree of the garden thou mayest freely eat: But of the tree of the knowledge of good and evil, thou shalt not eat of it: for in the day that thou eatest thereof thou shalt surely die. (Genesis 2:16-17)

Rules in Sports

For those of you who are athletic, or at least you try to be half-way coordinated on the field or court, you know that every game we play has rules. For those of you who never graced the field or court with your presence, you have likely played card or board games in your home. No matter which case applies to you, we all learned at an early age that every game has rules. When you are learning to play a sport or a game, the very first lessons you get are mostly about learning the rules. You will not become a good player unless you learn to apply the rules effectively to your game play. Once you know the rules, it is very easy to catch someone who tries to break the rules. We call that cheating. That is also why we have referees.

I love watching kids playing in pee-wee leagues because they really don't care about the score, they are just out to have fun, high-five all of the other players, and get a Popsicle after the game. Have you ever seen a kid run the wrong way on the football field or score a basket for the other team? It is just fun to watch kids learn. I remember when my son started playing soccer, it was very easy to tell where the ball was because every kid on the field was within ten feet of the ball. I have a picture from the local newspaper of my son playing T-Ball when he was five. He was playing first base the night this picture was taken. The picture shows him standing on the base with his mitt in front of his face talking to the player on the other team with no idea what was going on relative to the game. Of course, I was in the stands yelling at him to at least pay attention (the same thing all of the other parents are yelling)! My yelling was in vain, much like we treat God when He tries to remind us to pay attention.

Kids carry the basketball without dribbling, they all follow the ball on the soccer field, and they run the wrong way on the baseball field because they do not know the rules of the game. It doesn't take very long for them to learn, and they transition from having fun to being competitive. That competitive spirit sometimes drives them to break the rules just to score points. We do the same thing in our spiritual life. We break the rules to fit into a certain crowd or to get that next promotion hoping that we don't get caught by the ultimate referee who sees everything we do. Rules exist in every aspect of our lives, including our spirit.

Rules in Society

Have you ever used the wrong tool for a job just because it was the tool closest to you? This may be a surprise to some of you, most tools were designed to be used for a very specific purpose. There have been attempts to create "multi-tools" but having tried some of those, most do not work very well. A tool designed to do everything typically does nothing well. As an engineer, I have gained experience knowing that when I design something, I have the best guidance on how to use my product. The same can be said for most inventors, they know how their product is supposed to be used and what will happen if you try to use that product for a function which it was not designed. My wife has a habit of getting very nice screwdrivers from my woodshop to use as a hammer, a pry bar, a can opener, and a chisel. All of you guys out there can likely relate. This approach might work, but it may leave some marks and it really wreaks havoc on my tools.

God established moral rules for society. If you look closely at the Ten Commandments, the first four are about man's relationship to God, and the remaining six are about man's relationship with each other. In essence, these are rules for the proper existence of human society. Many think that God just created a bunch of rules so He could beat us into submission, control every move we make, and take all of the fun out of life. Now that I am officially a senior citizen, I have been around the block enough times to know that those commandments were made by the one who designed, created, and put us into production. The designer knows best how to establish the moral code needed for us to relate to Him and to each other. When we break these rules, we break our relationship with God, and we create a society full of chaos.

These moral codes are simply God telling us that human existence will be so much better if we just follow them. When we break these moral codes of conduct, there are negative consequences. Bad things begin to happen as a result. Just turn on the evening news, and you will see the direct results of not heeding the warning signs God established. It does not matter if we like the rules, but they are still the rules for proper human existence put in place by the creator of the human race.

What Rules Must We Keep According to God?

Many people today, including many that attend church weekly, no longer believe that the original Ten Commandments apply to our modern society. They were chiseled into stone tablets hundreds of years ago, and they were meant for a primitive society. I am a strong believer that a person claiming to be a Christian must believe the entire Word of God. You cannot pick and choose to follow just the parts you like. For that reason, we are going to briefly review the original Ten Commandments in the Old Testament to see where they fit into our society today by looking at a general description of each commandment. We will then take a look at how we violate that commandment today. Lastly, we will see the negative impact across society that results from breaking the commandment. I would recommend you go get a Bible and turn to the Book of Exodus, chapter 20 so you can read the words yourself. Here they are:

Commandment 1: (Ex. 20:3) Thou shalt have no Other Gods Before Me

God created mankind for the purpose of fellowship and friendship with Him. God created the entire universe in preparation for His ultimate creation, mankind. The very words in the first chapters of Genesis tell us that we are created in the image of God. We are His favorite creation. As you read the first chapters of the Bible, you will find that God came by the Garden of Eden every day to talk to Adam and Eve. God wanted His creation of free-will beings to choose to be His close friends. Adam and Eve had the opportunity for direct interface with God, and nothing else existed to distract them – until they disobeyed God's only command to them. God was first in their lives until they sinned.

You can find further confirmation of the fact that God intended on having direct fellowship with mankind by the comment that is made when God decided to destroy the world by flood. God's word says that every thought and imagination of man was evil and it "grieved" Him that He had made mankind. In other words, mankind completely forgot about God. We no longer even thought about Him. That broke His heart.

How do we Break This Commandment Today?

Our society is doing exactly what mankind did just before the great flood. We have no time for God, everything else comes before we spend any time with God in worship, in prayer or in studying His word. In essence, most people no longer even think about God unless some huge tragedy comes upon them. I remember very clearly the events of September 11, 2001. I can still tell you exactly where I was and what I was doing when the news stations began to play out the terrible events of that day. It was amazing that all of a sudden, it was okay to pray in school or on public property. No one was offended then! People that weekend went to church and you could feel a wave of patriotism and faith swell. It lasted about two weeks and our society was right back to normal.

As I am finishing this book now, we are living through the Coronavirus pandemic and the social travel restrictions now in place. I am locked in my house with my wife for the next four weeks, so we will see how this goes. Schools are closed, all of the sporting events are canceled, the restaurants are closed, movie theaters are closed, and only essential activities are supposed to be allowed. All extracurricular activities have been canceled, so all people have to do is stay home. We now have several weeks of time to spend at home with our families and just maybe to give thought to the pace of our current lives and what is really important. Churches are live streaming services since we cannot all have large public meetings, and I am noticing once again seems to be okay to pray and to talk about God. Knowing how we humans are, I am quite sure most will go right back to our busy lives and push God to the back burner once this virus has subsided. Oh, how quickly we forget God. Do you think this commandment is still valid today?

The Result of Breaking This Rule:

Our society has grown to think about God only in times of the most urgent need. As I mentioned above, we are living through this period of time with the Coronavirus Pandemic. As this pandemic first became a serious threat here in the United States, it instantly brought out the worst in some. People began hoarding supplies and food so they could resell them online at a huge price increase. Selfishness and greed were abundant at the expense of the elderly, infants, and those with underlying medical problems that were susceptible to this virus. I remember one story where a lady went to several local stores and purchased all of the disinfecting wipes and baby formula and then tried to sell them online for huge profits. Hundreds of similar stories permeated social media. This makes it very clear what happens when God is not first in our lives. We selfishly take first place even at the cost of everyone else around us.

If we are not thinking about God, His laws are not important to us. We are now in a society that is all about us. We have grown to become completely selfish, which can now easily be seen in our children. Everything has become all about "me" and what is in it for me. This attitude has caused most people today to turn away from helping others or just simply being kind. You want proof of this statement, just go out for a drive and see how long it is before someone yells at you, cuts you off, and gives you the old #1 sign with the wrong finger, or glares at you because you are driving too slowly. The result of breaking this commandment is that mankind has put ourselves as number one, we are selfish, proud, and unkind to others. Do you remember what Satan said to Eve as part of the reason to eat the fruit from the forbidden tree? He said this will "make you wise just like God." We removed God and put ourselves in His place and we no longer even think about Him.

Commandment 2: (Ex 20: 4-6) Thou Shalt not Make a Graven Image or Worship Idols

As you read this commandment, you might be thinking "Hey, I don't worship some statue or some person here on earth." That may be a true statement, but if you take this to the heart of the commandment, it tells me that ANYTHING that takes the place of God in your life is an idol. It can be your house, your car, your job, your sport, your hobby, or maybe even a special person. God is very clear here that He must take first place in your life. The second commandment is joined closely to the first commandment. Verse five makes this summary accurate because God says He is a jealous God and does not to share you with anything else. Do you remember your first real crush on some boy or girl? I am sure then you will also remember the day that they found someone they liked more than you. Do you remember how that felt? That is exactly what God is saying to us in this commandment. He wants us to love Him more than ANYTHING else.

How do we Break this Commandment Today?

We do not give God any of our time. We are so busy today with life that we have shoved God completely out of our hearts and minds. When I was growing up in the 1960s and 1970s, I remember us having to buy gas and groceries on Saturday because nothing was open on Sunday. There definitely were no school events on Sunday. In addition to that, there were no school functions on Wednesday nights so people could go to church on Bible study nights through the week. Where are we today when it comes to giving God our time? Everything else takes priority. We sign our kids up to play travel ball, or regional gymnastics, or robotic competitions that all occur over the entire weekend, including Sunday. What happened to Wednesday evenings? That is typically the hardest practice for the big game on Friday night. Our professional sports play on Sundays. The big auto races are now on Sundays. This list could go on for a few pages. The bottom line, all of these *things* have taken God's place. They have become our idols. What about our jobs? We are willing to work seventy or eighty hours a week to pay for a new car, your new big house, or a Disney vacation, but we are too tired to do the work of the church for God. All of our "stuff" today has taken God's place, and it has become our idol. This is exactly how Satan is defeating most Christians today. He has us living with attitudes of self-gratification, so we spend all of our time on ourselves. Again, we have put ourselves above God.

The Result of Breaking This Rule:

God has been completely forced out of our lives by our desire for more things, popularity, that next promotion, a desire to be popular, or maybe have a title with your name. Very simply put, we are super-selfish and too busy to think about our eternal soul. The stress level of our society is likely at its highest point ever. As we are driven to obtain more stuff, we begin to crumble under the weight of keeping pace with everyone else. It has led to a society with an enormous substance abuse problem. The rural area where I live now has one of the worst opioid addiction problems of any region in the country. Alcohol destroys more families and takes more lives today than ever before. So, what has breaking this commandment done to us? We are now a self-destructive society. That is just what Satan wants, and we are playing right into his plan.

Commandment 3: (Ex. 20:7) Thou Shalt not Take the Name of the Lord in Vain

You may not think you have an issue with this topic because you don't curse. I need to ask you, how many times do you say "Oh, my god," or how many times do you just repeat the name of God even in church and you are just repeating it over and over? Paul tells the church we are not to pray with "vain repetitions." This commandment is all about having a very Holy respect for God's name and for us to choose carefully the words we speak. Most people in our society today do not think a moment about letting foul language come from their mouth, especially cursing while using God's name. How many of you have heard someone yell out "god" or "Jesus" and it is not in a good way? That is what we are talking about here.

How Do We Break this Commandment Today?

Foul language today is not just a problem; it is an epidemic. Most of the shows and even the cartoons today are filled with foul language. All you have to do is turn on the TV today, and you will hear vulgar speech. Go to local schools and you will hear vulgar speech. Go to your local ballpark or sporting event and you will hear vulgar language. Worst of all, our very households are full of grandparents, parents, and kids yelling and screaming vulgar language. We have created a generation of people that have minimal respect for others.

The Result of Breaking this Rule:

We no longer have a holy reverence for God's name. As I told you the story of the young child that dropped the "F-bomb" at the church daycare, our children are now so accustomed to hearing foul and vulgar language that it's become part of everyday life. It no longer bothers people to use inappropriate words regardless of the setting or environment.

I remember an experience I witnessed that goes to the heart of this issue. I was in line at the ticket counter of an airline terminal, and the weather was bad outside. Flights were being delayed. There was a man who became so irate, that he was literally screaming at the ticketing agent with such profanity that it was shameful. Everyone within fifty feet could hear this guy. It did not matter that it was a weather delay, the man took out his frustration and hatred on a poor lady at the ticket counter. Over my many years out in the public, I have witnessed scenes like this numerous times and I notice the frequency and intensity seem to be increasing as our society becomes more self-centered. Most people today are all about "telling you what they think" and how dare you get in their way or disagree with them. Most people today feel it is their right to blow their top and spew whatever words they feel like saying regardless of who might hear them. They call it "being honest." What is even worse, some of those people I have heard spew out the vulgar language attend church on Sunday mornings. Jesus said that bitter and sweet water cannot come from the same well. This is what has happens when we violate this commandment, our words become poison. Could you imagine a society today where no one used foul language? Do you think this commandment should apply today?

Commandment 4: (Ex 20:8-10) Remember the Sabbath Day, to keep it holy. Six days shalt thou labour, and do all thy work: But the seventh day is the sabbath of the LORD thy God: in it thou shalt not do any work, thou, nor thy son, nor thy daughter, thy manservant, nor thy maidservant, nor thy cattle, nor thy stranger that is within thy gates:

I am not going into much detail on this one because the purpose of this book is not to have a debate about whether we should worship God on Saturday or Sunday. This is the only one of the original Ten Commandments that is not repeated in the New Testament. Based upon what Jesus said about the Sabbath day, we must address the intent of this commandment for us today. In Mark 2:27, we have guidance from Jesus related to this commandment:

> *And he said unto them, The sabbath was made for man, and not man for the sabbat.* (Mark 2:27 KJV)

In the book of Colossians, Paul tells the church:

> *Let no man therefore judge you in meat, or in drink,*
> *or in respect of an holyday, or of the new moon, or*
> *of the sabbath days.* (Colossians 2:16 KJV)

The religious leaders of Jesus' day had turned this command-ment, which includes doing no work on the Sabbath, into reli-gious dogma. The intent of the commandment is for us to rest from our day-to-day work and cares of life for one day and we are to honor and worship God during that time of rest. This way, our minds stay focused on God and not the cares of this life. Have you ever received a phone call from someone and you did not recognize their voice because you have not heard from them in a very long time? Most of the time, if someone like that calls, it is because they want something. Do you see where I am going with this spiritually? The only time most people have for God today is when they are really in trouble; they never talk to Him any other time because they just don't have time for God.

God does not want us distracted from our interaction with Him. That is why we are told to enter into our closet to pray (Matt. 6:6) so that God has our undivided attention. God knows how easily we are distracted as humans, and that is why He just asks us to set aside some time to only think about Him. The time or day you chose to do this is totally between you and God, but you need to do it, and it takes discipline.

How do we Break it Today?

We have already discussed earlier under the second command-ment, the fact that society has completely done away with our dedicated times that use to be set aside for God. Simply put, when we do not set aside recurring specific time to commune with God, negative results will follow. We don't want to go to church, we don't want to study God's Word, we don't take quiet time to pray and talk to God, and we most definitely do not talk about Him to our friends and family. Our society today has filled their Sundays with trips and sporting events. Rather we're showing our children that taking time for God and attending church is less important than going to the ballgame. How can God minister to us and teach us if we never spend time with Him? We break this commandment every time we choose to push God out of our lives.

The Result of Breaking this Rule:

We have come so far away from giving time to God that even many of our churches no longer have service on Sunday nights. Most of the people who claim to be Christians in America will not even give God two hours on Sunday. I am pretty confident that if people do not even come back to church on Sunday evenings, I know they are not taking time to read their Bible or pray through the week. There is one church in our area that canceled their services on Sunday nights, so those attending their church can have family time. You might be thinking to yourself that is not a bad thing but wake up, we have six other days that God gave us to have family time, but we have filled it with everything under the sun so we take time allotted for God to stay home and watch TV. If I were a betting person, most of those people attending that church do not have family time on Sunday nights, they are out at some event, watching TV, or on their cell phones. Would I be correct? Breaking this rule makes it easier for us to forget about God. If He does not get any of your dedicated time, then there will be a huge hole in the eternal part of your being.

Satan will be sure that hole is filled by the world and you will lose your eternal connection to God.

You might ask the question, "If this commandment is not repeated in the New Testament, then do we still have to keep it?" All I am going to do is give you two verses of scripture and let you decide for yourself:

> *Not forsaking the assembling of ourselves together, as the manner of some is; but exhorting one another: and so much the more, as ye see the day approaching.* (Hebrews 10:25 KJV)

> *But thou, when thou prayest, enter into thy closet, and when thou hast shut thy door, pray to thy Father which is in secret; and thy Father which seeth in secret shall reward thee openly.* (Matthew 6:6 KJV)

I think God wants us to spend some dedicated time with Him.

Commandment 5: (Ex 20:12) Honor thy Father and Mother

I am not even sure where to start with this commandment. It is the first commandment that has to do with our relationships here on earth. Proper relationships here on earth start in your home with the family unit. I grew up in a very strict home (and I am now glad for that), so straying away from honoring father and mother was not really an option. I know what it is to be raised in a strict family unit and I also know what it is to raise a child of my own in the society we have today. I was always taught to respect my parents. I didn't always like what they said, nor did I like living by their rules, but disrespecting my parents was NOT an option. If I ever did, there were immediate consequences. What I see today in full public view is a blatant disrespect for parents. I saw one video on YouTube where a teenager was in Walmart and laying on the floor, throwing a temper tantrum because his parent would not buy them a video game. I can only imagine what would have happened to me had I done something like that as a kid in public. I probably wouldn't be writing this book today. My wife and I raised our son in a strict home, where he was taught to respect others and to love God. He turned out *great*. This approach does work.

As a Christian, I see this is the tip of the spear in the spiritual war today in America. The family unit has been under intense attack beginning with the removal of prayer from schools in the early 1960s and continues today. The enemy knows that if he can get our kids to stay away from God, he will be successful in tearing apart society. There is a record of Adolph Hitler saying that all he needed to do was train the kids to change society. Do you see where that ended? Hollywood, the media, and many of our politicians are carrying out open warfare on the traditional family unit under the disguise of political correctness and inclusiveness. Our children today are being raised in a society that is even trying to convince them they should not even be a boy or a girl. If you claim to be a Christian or a religious person of any affiliation, all you have to do is watch the most recent shows and commercials to realize there is a very clear agenda in almost everything you now see on TV.

How do we Break this Commandment Today? This one is pretty easy to understand; it is disrespect for parents, guardians, and the elderly in general. Treating these categories of individuals like second class citizens, pushing them out of the way (physically and emotionally), and taking advantage of them violates God's law. If we cannot even respect our earthly parents that took care of us and raised us, how can we love and respect God that we cannot see?

The Result of Breaking this Rule:

Breaking this commandment is not only a critical breakdown in the basic family unit, but it has led our society to an accompanying disrespect for the elderly in general. At the pace we are moving, it will not be long before older people are deemed little value to society, a drain on healthcare, and a danger on the highways, so let's just let them die off faster.

Commandment 6: (Ex 20:13) Thou shalt not kill

This one also needs little explanation. We do not have the right to take another human life for absolutely no reason. As I read the Bible from Old Testament to New Testament, there are times when taking a life is unavoidable, such as a time of war or in a time of self-defense when you or your family's life is in imminent danger. Even under these exceptions, I believe there are still times when killing may be unnecessary. These are general exceptions to the basic rule, but outside of those, God tells us we do not have the right to take the life of another human.

How do we break this commandment today?

Throughout history, man has waged war and killed each other from the very first two children born on earth, Cain and Abel. Our society has roaming gangs in areas that simply kill for the sake of killing. We have thieves that kill for even the smallest amount of money. We have some people who create new and more violent ways to kills others.

This also applies to the attack currently ongoing in America against our unborn children. Our society has labeled it "freedom of choice," and many call it abortion, but no matter what term you assign to this act, it is murder. A recent statement from a Pro-Choice representative said, "Pro-choice is similar to having a colonoscopy or a tooth pulled." The most offensive is late-trimester or partial-birth abortion. We can be fined and imprisoned for killing a bald eagle, but we can execute late-term children and call it free-choice. Human life no longer has value. We can discard the remains of a child along with the waste and trash without any feeling of remorse.

The Result of Breaking this Rule:

The value of human life has become practically meaningless. We, as a society, have become almost numb to hearing about assaults and murders. Nothing surprises us anymore. As long as it happens somewhere else, we no longer seem to really care. Since America has been at war against terrorism for nearly 20 years, we are seeing many of our soldiers return from combat with PTSD. Killing or seeing death has a strong negative impact on a person, even in times of war. As a participant and supporter of the Ride-2-Recovery and Wounded Warrior Projects, I have witnessed the impact of war on our nation's veterans. When human life becomes of no value, it gives way to the rise of governments that commit atrocities like genocide and ethnic cleansing because, in their eyes, most humans are worthless. This low value of life is what gives way to slavery, human trafficking, and substance abuse to the extreme. The majority of the world stands idly by and watches.

Commandment 7: (Ex 20:14) Thou shalt not commit adultery

Because of an incident that happened to me as a Sunday School teacher, I am going to start this section with simple definitions from the Random House College Dictionary First Edition 1975:

Adultery: voluntary sexual intercourse of a married person with someone other than his or her lawful spouse.

Fornication: voluntary sexual intercourse between two unmarried persons or two persons not married to each other.

For the sake of information, I want to include how Jesus Himself defined adultery in the New Testament:

> *Ye have heard that it was said by them of old time, Thou shalt not commit adultery: But I say unto you, That whosoever looketh on a woman to lust after her hath committed adultery with her already in his heart.* (Matthew 5:27-28)

This commandment is all about being true to your spouse and only having sexual relationships with your spouse. This commandment also addresses another term that we don't hear very often and that is "fornication." In very simple terms, God says do NOT cheat on your spouse or have inappropriate sexual relationships to a person to who you are not legally married.

I remember the vows I took thirty-four years ago, when my wife and I got married. I remember the minister saying, "for better or for worse, for richer for poorer, in sickness and in health, until death do us part." To me, this was serious business when

I said, "I do." I am sure my wife will tell you there are many times she would like to have taken me out, but we have made it through those through times because we are committed to each other, and those vows were our foundation.

This commandment addresses one of the biggest issues facing America and likely one of the biggest problems inside the church of America today. Statistics show that nearly 50% of all marriages end in divorce today. Why is that? Once again, the constant attack against the family unit and the lack of commitment between men and women today have caused us to think we can just walk away from a marriage at the first signs of a challenge. Some of us bail on marriage if we see someone else come along that we desire more than our current spouse. We just walk away like there's been no commitment. We have church leaders committing adultery and still, getting up to preach every Sunday morning as though they are doing no wrong. In our current society of acceptance and inclusion, we are fearful of taking a stand about the definition of marriage as God defines it. So, this may not be a politically correct statement, but God clearly defined marriage as that between a man and a woman. Here are the Words of Jesus on this topic:

> *And He answered and said to them, "Have you not read that He who made them at the beginning 'made them male and female,' and said, 'For this reason a man shall leave his father and mother and be joined to his wife, and the two shall become one flesh'? So then, they are no longer two but one flesh. Therefore what God has joined together, let not man separate."* (Matthew 19:4-6 NKJV)

I don't know how much clearer God can define marriage. If you have a concern with this definition, you need to take that up with God because these are the words of Jesus Christ Himself. I just copied them here for you to read. Sexual relationships outside of this definition break this commandment.

How do we Break it Today?

The problem many people have with this commandment is that we all want to live in a society where we can fulfill all of the lust and desire but still call ourselves Christians. We do this because we are redefining marriage from what God said to what we want it to say. You cannot call yourself a Christian and willfully and intentionally break God's law.

> *Nevertheless the solid foundation of God stands, having this seal: "The Lord knows those who are His," and, "Let everyone who names the name of Christ depart from iniquity." (2 Timothy 2:19 NKJV)*

Here are some of the things we do as a society and even inside the church that are a direct violation of this commandment: We "shack up" or just move in with someone outside of marriage; we have little rendezvous with a coworker you really like and your spouse is unaware. We send little flirty texts with someone other than our spouse; we think it is okay to have sexual relationships with multiple people, and yes, same-sex marriage falls into this area. If you read through the books in the New Testament that Paul wrote to the churches, you will find that nearly every book mentions that the church members struggled with this sin and Paul said to avoid it. This is a pretty clear indication this sin has a foothold in the church and how much more out in the unsaved world?

The Result of Breaking this Rule:

As stated above, nearly 50% of all marriages in the United States today end in divorce. The primary reason the divorce rate has recently leveled off is because people are just not getting married today. Many today just move in together and cohabitate with no legal commitment. There is no longer the lifetime commitment necessary that holds families together. Coupled with Commandment #5 to honor our parents, breaking this commandment is further deterioration of the family. The family unit as God established with the first humans has been ripped apart by modern society. Many today have taken the easy road by moving in with each other and then part ways at the first sign of problems. That may seem okay for adults, but what then happens to all of the children now caught up in this situation.

As my wife runs a large daycare, she has shared the direct impact this has on the children. Different people come to pick children up; they spend weekends with different parents; they have to split up holidays like Christmas and Thanksgiving. However, the worst part is they hear their parents fight and talk bad about each other. Our children then witness these actions and that is how they think a family is supposed to be. If you think the breakup of the family does not impact the children, you are incorrect. The bottom line is that our children are paying a high price in their level of stress. Children's illnesses increase, they act out in rebellion to get attention and, as they grow, they play the parents off of each other. The cycle then continues with each generation getting worse. Adults, we are the problem because we are more concerned with having our little fun with a *new person* when we get tired of the old one. We just trade them off like a used car.

You might call me old fashioned on this one, but the results of breaking this commandment are hitting us in the face every day. All you need to do is go out in public or watch the news. The ultimate result of breaking this commandment has become the destruction of our families.

To show you how far even the church has strayed on this commandment, I have to share an incident that happened to me as a Sunday school teacher. I had someone ask me if it was okay just to move in with another person without getting married. What surprised me the most was that they were an older couple that had been raised in church. They just didn't think they needed to go through the legal action of getting married because society now says you don't really need to get married. They knew what God's Word says, but they didn't think it applied to them.

Commandment 8: (Ex 20:15) Thou shalt not steal

Stealing is taking something that does not belong to you. Pretty simple to define, but you may be surprised how far-reaching this commandment is in our lives.

How do we Break it Today?

We have no regard for the property of other people. Just park your car in a lot at a large store, and people will open their doors against your car, leave a mark and walk away. Look at the trash along the highway and in your yard along the street. People no longer care. We also take things that do not belong to us by not being honest. Have you ever been given too much change back at a store and you knowingly kept it? Have you ever "gamed" the system to benefit yourself and not pay your taxes? Has someone done work for you and you didn't fully pay them? Have you ever overcharged someone for a job? Have you ever used something and then taken it back and claimed it didn't work right after you completed your job? Have you ever eaten most of a meal and then claimed there was a hair in your meal so you could get it free? Here is one that many who attend church will not like, do you give 100% at your job? Do you goof off at work? Do you cause trouble with your coworkers, or cheat on your time? Do you take office supplies from work? I could keep going with this list but by now you should get the point. You see, all of these things condition us to think it is okay to take things that do not belong to us because they are just small things and the company will never miss them. Stop and think that as more people do this, the cost to the company becomes very large. Guess what the companies then do? They charge more for their products. Bottom line, you will pay for it anyway.

The Result of Breaking this Rule:

There was a time not so long ago when we didn't have to lock our homes or cars. Now we have digital video surveillance systems, alarms, and sensors that monitor our homes while we are gone. I have personally experienced, and an attempted break-in of my house. I have had a very nice stereo system stolen from the dashboard of my vehicle. You become a victim and your property has been violated.

We now spend hundreds of dollars on monitoring equipment and service. What about those who steal your identify, image your phone, or hack your credit cards and bank account?

Breaking this commandment is costing all of us lots of money. The price you pay for goods and services increases to cover the cost of theft. Many of the big chain stores no longer even prosecute people that are caught stealing merchandise from the store. Breaking this commandment has resulted in an epidemic theft problem..

Commandment 9: (Ex 20:16) Thou shalt not bear false witness

False witness is another term for lying or not telling the truth. There is also another word that needs to be mentioned here with this commandment, and that is the word deceit. If you have children, do you ever remember sitting down and teaching them how to lie? Likely not, so where did they learn how to lie? Our children learn very quickly from the examples they see every day.

How do we Break this Rule Today?

Listen to our news outlets, listen to our politicians, listen to crafty salespeople, and listen to those caught in the act of committing crimes lying to the police officer. It is almost impossible to trust anyone anymore. Have you ever purchased a product that claimed to do something that it really would not do but they offered a 100% money-back guarantee? There was likely some requirement written is super fine print that canceled out your refund. They lied and they knew it.

Have you ever been on the receiving end of a scam or super high-pressure sales tactics? What about defaulting on a loan? We likely knew we couldn't pay for the item we wanted but we got it, used it, then let it go back without paying for it in full.

Have you lied to try to get out of a traffic ticket? Have you lied at work to cover for not doing your job correctly or making a mistake? Did you blame something on a coworker when it was just as much your fault for the failure? Did you blame a team member in a sporting event for causing you to lose? I could just keep going with this list, so I hope you see how far we have allowed lying to creep into our daily lives. We no longer even give it a thought. It has become a way of life.

The Result of Breaking this Rule:

We cannot believe nearly any of what we read or hear today. Any information from the large companies selling products, the media, or our politicians is questionable at best. Did you ever wonder why we have to sign so much paperwork today when we make a major purchase? What about the dramatic increase in the number of lawyers needed to administer agreements and contracts? Why is that? Because we cannot trust anyone today. Agreements use to be made on a handshake because individuals were trustworthy and would follow through with their agreements. Today, most people will do what they can to find a loophole or simply just not abide by their word or commitment. Our society is paying a very high price monetarily because of the because of the overwhelming level of deceit that exists.

The consequences also bleed over into our relationships and spiritual lives. We will tell a lie to get us out of situations that might bring embarrassment to us. We will lie to make ourselves look good, and we will lie to get what we want even at the expense of others. This pervasive attitude of lying has caused many to not trust anyone, including God. It is a clear indication of our spiritual condition deep in our lives because all lies originate from Satan

Ye are of your father the devil, and the lusts of your father ye will do. He was a murderer from the beginning, and abode not in the truth, because there is no truth in him. When he speaketh a lie, he speaketh of his own: for he is a liar, and the father of it. (John 8:44 KJV)

Commandment 10: (Ex 20:17) Thou shalt not covet

This commandment is about the desire and lust for material or physical things. Coveting under this commandment means that you want something so bad you will do whatever it takes to get it. An example list of things not to covet are: houses, servants, spouses, animals, or any other property that belongs to someone else. This covers about everything you can imagine.

Here are some scriptures from the New Testament that are associated with this commandment:

But godliness with contentment is great gain. For we brought nothing into this world, and it is certain we can carry nothing out. And having food and raiment let us be therewith content. But they that will be rich fall into temptation and a snare, and into many foolish and hurtful lusts, which drown men in destruction and perdition. For the love of money is the root of all evil: which while some coveted after, they have erred from the faith, and pierced themselves through with many sorrows. (1 Timothy 6:6-10)

*Let your conversation be without covetousness;
and be content with such things as ye have: for he
hath said, I will never leave thee, nor forsake thee.*
(Hebrews 13:5)

How do we Break the Rule Today?

We want the best. We want just as much as everyone around us, and we want it immediately. We take most of our time acquiring more things and then those things take more of our time to upkeep and retain. I will just throw out an example to give you an idea of what is happening in our society today. When we voluntarily work overtime at our job so we can obtain that new car, boat, motorcycle, wardrobe, pair of shoes, tool, vacation, etc., because we cannot afford it on our standard income, that is breaking this commandment. You might be saying, "Now wait a minute, how does working extra hours to buy something break this commandment?" You have traded those working hours most likely for time you should have gone to church, read your Bible, prayed, or at least spent with your family. This desire to have more has us in a mode of working so that we can keep up with the neighbors, live in that huge house, drive that new car, wear the latest designer clothing, or sit in the corner office at work. We are willing to do whatever it takes, even at the expense of our spiritual walk.

The Result of Breaking this Rule:

Our recent generations of people have become spoiled. We spend most of our lives piling up *things*. There is a saying that goes, "He who dies with the most toys, wins." Have you noticed how many storage facilities are being built in America today? The demand for more is ever increasing. Most of us have way more than we will ever need. Considering a large majority of the world's population survives on $2.50/day, we will spend more than that on a cup of coffee and complain if it is not hot enough for us. We are now all about convenience for ourselves. I have watched those around me become completely consumed with working multiple jobs so they can buy their kids the clothes with the most famous logos. We have become a very selfish society, and we are teaching our next generation of children that this is the way life is supposed to be. The desire for more has caused us to be totally consumed with material assets and our position in the local community at the expense of our families and our spiritual lives.

> *As he came forth of his mother's womb, naked shall he return to go as he came, and shall take nothing of his labour, which he may carry away in his hand.* (Ecclesiastes 5:15 KJV)

> *But godliness with contentment is great gain. For we brought nothing into this world, and it is certain we can carry nothing out. And having food and raiment let us be therewith content. But they that will be rich fall into temptation and a snare, and into many foolish and hurtful lusts, which drown men in destruction and perdition. For the love of money is the root of all evil: which while some coveted after, they have erred from the faith, and pierced themselves through with many sorrows.* (1 Timothy 6:6-10 KJV)

God wants us to be content with what He has given us. He said He would supply all of our needs according to His riches in glory through Christ Jesus.

Do These Commandments Apply Today?

At this point, you should see how these commandments still apply to us today. I listed some of the New Testament scriptures as you read through the basic commandments, but I felt it necessary to list a few more to support my assessment that the Ten Commandments still apply today as God's standard for defining good. For those that say the Ten Commandments are in the Old Testament of the Bible and do not apply to us today, here are some additional scriptures in the New Testament that Jesus and Paul said about the rules we must keep:

> *And Jesus answered him, The first of all the commandments is, Hear, O Israel; The Lord our God is one Lord: And thou shalt love the Lord thy God with all thy heart, and with all thy soul, and with all thy mind, and with all thy strength: this is the first commandment. And the second is like, namely this, Thou shalt love thy neighbour as thyself. There is none other commandment greater than these.* (Mark 12:29-31 KJV)

> *And, behold, one came and said unto him, Good Master, what good thing shall I do, that I may have eternal life? And he said unto him, Why callest thou me good? There is none good but one, that is, God: but if thou wilt enter into life, keep the commandments. He saith unto him, Which? Jesus said, Thou shalt do no murder, Thou shalt not commit adultery, Thou shalt not steal, Thou shalt not bear false witness, Honour thy father and thy mother: and, Thou shalt love thy neighbour as thyself. The young man saith unto him, All these*

things have I kept from my youth up: what lack I yet? Jesus said unto him, If thou wilt be perfect, go and sell that thou hast, and give to the poor, and thou shalt have treasure in heaven: and come and follow me. (Matthew 19:16-21 KJV)

For this, Thou shalt not commit adultery, Thou shalt not kill, Thou shalt not steal, Thou shalt not bear false witness, Thou shalt not covet; and if there be any other commandment, it is briefly comprehended in this saying, namely, Thou shalt love thy neighbour as thyself. (Romans 13:9 KJV)

You might be saying to yourself after reading all of this about the Ten Commandments that this is pretty heavy stuff... and it is. The reason for laying this out to you is that there is a direct connection to these commandments and what we call being *good*. If we break these most basic rules God gave us, then you cannot be good enough to be allowed into His Kingdom in the future. There must be consequences that follow broken rules.

God Sets Boundaries

The old saying, "The grass is always greener on the other side of the fence" seems to apply to animals and people. We raised several animals on our farm including cattle and pigs. It always amazed me that I carried food and water to the animals, cleaned out their pens, put them inside shelter in bad weather, and provided medicine when they were sick... but every time I left the gate open, they got out. Animals almost always go outside the boundaries, no matter how good you treat them. People have done the same thing to God. He cares for all of our needs and wants us to spend eternity with Him, but we cannot stay inside of the boundaries He has set.

These rules that we call a moral code of conduct were given as part of being a creature that has a free will. Free will comes with boundaries and God has provided them in His Word and His Son lived them while He was here on earth. God also warns us of the consequences for breaking these rules.

> *Think not that I am come to destroy the law, or the prophets: I am not come to destroy, but to fulfil.* (Matthew 5:17 KJV)

Other Questions to Consider

- Are you clear about God's rules, even though society does not like some of them?
- What negative events do you see in your life that were a result of breaking God's rules?
- What are you to do when mankind's laws are in direct conflict with God's Laws?

Chapter 5

Consequences for Breaking God's Rules

But of the tree of the knowledge of good and evil,
thou shalt not eat of it: for in the day that thou
eatest thereof thou shalt surely die. (Genesis 2:17)

I wanted to begin this chapter by talking about the original rule God gave to Adam and Eve in the Garden of Eden. As a Sunday school teacher for more than thirty-five years, I have heard people ask the question, why did God even make rules especially one that just says they couldn't eat from a tree and oh, by the way, the penalty for eating from the tree was death, isn't that just a little harsh? It does not take a Ph.D. in theology or psychology to answer this question. God wanted our human life to be very simple, yet give mankind a real choice. Basically, mankind began existence here on earth with just a single, simple rule that had the purpose of testing obedience, yet allowing a free will. You do not see a long list of rules like don't kill, don't steal, don't lie, etc. Mankind was just like our kids playing pee-wee leagues, Adam and Eve were innocent, however, they were created to have a free will. This single, simple rule not to eat from one tree was given just so mankind had the free choice to obey God or not.

As you read this one verse that clearly defines the rule, God was also very clear that if that rule is broken, there would be consequences. If your childhood was anything like mine, I know you heard the phrase, "If I have to stop this car, I am going to (fill in the blank)." The one parent phrase I know will likely bring shivers to your body is "you just wait until we get home!"

Bad choices result in bad consequences.

The Dryer

It has been such a joy to raise a son and in the early days of our son's life, we got pretty good at playing tricks on each other. Now most ladies are afraid of critters like bugs, frogs, spiders, and snakes, but my son took scaring mom to a new level. Almost every young boy has (or can get) fake critters. Well, my son had more than a few, and he would place them around the house in hidden locations only to be found by an unsuspecting parent – usually his mom. One specific trick I will remember was when my son wanted to scare his mom with one of those fake critters. He obviously planned this one out well in advance because he managed to put a large rubber snake in the dryer with a load of laundry. Needless to say, when my wife got about halfway through folding that load as she pulled out a shirt, that rubber snake came out in a hurry and landed right on her. The good thing for my son was he just happened to be at school or I think he might be about three inches shorter than he is today. Needless to say, there were consequences when he got home. I am still laughing, even as I tell this story again.

Our society does not want to face the fact that the God who cre-ated this universe will implement the consequences if we dis-obey His rules. Just like for the first humans, God has given us advance warning about the results of disobeying Him, yet we choose to disobey anyway. How do we react? We blame Him for the consequences. Consequences mean there is account-ability. As we discussed earlier, about the internal moral code, the driving force behind the "progressive" agenda today is to remove God from every aspect of our society. If you remove God, you remove the rules. If there is no God, then there is no one to hold us accountable for breaking the moral code. Just like when our parents delivered the consequences to us as kids, it is a fearful thing to think about the fact that at some point in the future, there will be consequences for disobedience applied by the one who created the universe. These consequences are not temporary, they are eternal.

One very effective way to learn is by making mistakes. Why is it that we seem to really learn better through mistakes? Could it be that mistakes typically have immediate, and most of the time, negative consequences? How many times have you heard or said, "Boy, I learned a hard lesson from that experience, I will never do that again"? I believe the main reason we learn so much from our mistakes is because we realize that it was our own conscious choices that resulted in the consequences. Bottom line: our choice caused the negative results. Now, this isn't an all-encompassing statement - sometimes we are put in a position that is not always our fault. But I would bet that even in those cases, if you look deep enough, you made a choice along the way that landed you in that position which could have been avoided by alternate choice.

The previous chapter describes the result of breaking God's commandments today. We need to be sure we understand that God is very clear about the results of living a sinful life. He does not approve of such and He tells us to expect His response when we willingly chose to disobey Him.

> *For if we sin wilfully after that we have received the knowledge of the truth, there remaineth no more sacrifice for sins.* (Hebrews 10:26)

We witness so many people today who attend church and claim to be Christians, yet willfully choose to break God's laws. According to God's Word, Christians and sin are incompatible. I am not sure people understand that when they call themselves Christian, they are claiming that they are ambassadors of Jesus Christ. They are taking His name and applying it to themselves. If we claim His name and willfully choose to violate His commandments, then we are taking His name in vain and dragging His name down to our level. If we break His commandments, then we should expect His response without surprise.

Did your parents ever forget about your bad behavior on the long trip home from some event, letting you get away with your errant ways? That only happened to me a few times as Mom and Dad might get distracted by some other topic and forget to follow through with the disciplinary actions for my bad behavior. I believe today, when God shows His mercy to us when we goof up, sometimes, we think we got away with our poor choice - but please remember, there is a record of our actions being recorded in Heaven. Mom and Dad may have forgotten, but God does not until we ask Him for His forgiveness. Even in His forgiveness, there will many times still be consequences, or we will not learn our lesson. We have unruly children today because parents have become lazy and not followed through with proper discipline when rules are broken. This ultimately leads to a selfish and spoiled society, which is proven by the bad behavior of most children today. God is not like the parents we have today. God has told us in advance of the consequences of our sin, so we have no excuse. Let's see how clear God was with Adam and Eve.

> *And the LORD God called unto Adam, and said unto him, Where art thou? And he said, I heard thy voice in the garden, and I was afraid, because I was naked; and I hid myself. And he said, Who told thee that thou wast naked? Hast thou eaten of the tree, whereof I commanded thee that thou shouldest not eat? And the man said, The woman whom thou gavest to be with me, she gave me of the tree, and I did eat. And the LORD God said unto the woman, What is this that thou hast done? And the woman said, The serpent beguiled me, and I did eat. And the LORD God said unto the serpent, Because thou hast done this, thou art cursed above all cattle, and above every beast of the field; upon thy belly shalt thou go, and dust shalt thou eat all the days of thy life: And I will put enmity between thee and the woman, and between thy seed and her seed; it shall bruise thy head, and thou shalt bruise his heel. Unto the woman he said, I will greatly multiply thy sorrow and thy conception; in sorrow thou shalt bring forth children; and thy desire shall be to thy husband, and he shall rule over thee. And unto Adam he said, Because thou hast hearkened unto the voice of thy wife, and hast eaten of the tree, of which I commanded*

thee, saying, Thou shalt not eat of it: cursed is the ground for thy sake; in sorrow shalt thou eat of it all the days of thy life; Thorns also and thistles shall it bring forth to thee; and thou shalt eat the herb of the field; In the sweat of thy face shalt thou eat bread, till thou return unto the ground; for out of it wast thou taken: for dust thou art, and unto dust shalt thou return. (Genesis 3:9-19)

And the LORD God said, Behold, the man is become as one of us, to know good and evil: and now, lest he put forth his hand, and take also of the tree of life, and eat, and live for ever: Therefore the LORD God sent him forth from the garden of Eden, to till the ground from whence he was taken. So he drove out the man; and he placed at the east of the garden of Eden Cherubims, and a flaming sword which turned every way, to keep the way of the tree of life. (Genesis 3:22-24)

Reading these scriptures tells me very clearly that God means what He says when it comes to the consequences of disobedience. God didn't go easy on Adam and Eve, He followed through with what He said He would do. The description God gave of the consequences are being lived out by each one of us to this day. God is serious about consequences for breaking His rules.

Man never got back into the garden because we disobeyed God.

Other Questions to Consider

- Is God too harsh on us for breaking His Commandments?
- Do you ask God for forgiveness and then go back and commit the same sin repeatedly?

Chapter 6

Accountability

As a supervisor for many years in industry, I noticed that most people have lost the sense of being held accountable for decisions they make or actions they carry out. Whenever anything bad happens, we quickly look to place the blame on someone else or on some external circumstance that caused the problem. Very few times will you ever hear the words "it was my fault." Placing blame on someone else began with the very first man and woman in the Garden of Eden.

> *And he said, Who told thee that thou wast naked? Hast thou eaten of the tree, whereof I commanded thee that thou shouldest not eat? And the man said, The woman whom thou gavest to be with me, she gave me of the tree, and I did eat. And the LORD God said unto the woman, What is this that thou hast done? And the woman said, The serpent beguiled me, and I did eat.* (Genesis 3:11-13 KJV)

Can you imagine the daily interactions and conversations Adam and Eve must have had with God? I am only speculating here, but I am guessing each day at about the same time, Adam and

Eve would come running up to the designated spot to talk to God just like children running to meet their parents and give them a hug. When Adam and Eve ate from that tree, the daily visit with God changed drastically. When God came down for His daily visit, He already knew something was not right because neither Adam nor Eve came to meet Him. They, too, already knew they were in trouble. Just like children who have done something wrong, they try to conceal their actions and hide. We all know that typically does not work well for us.

Notice God didn't yell at Adam and Eve or immediately condemn them; He simply started asking questions until they told on themselves. How many of you can remember a time when your parents simply said, "what have you done?" Isn't it interesting that most of the time our parents already knew we had disobeyed but they wanted us to own up for whatever disobedient behavior we had done. This is called accountability. We cannot hide our disobedience from God.

Just like children, Adam first blamed Eve. In fact, if you read the verses above carefully, you will see that Adam insinuated that it was God's fault for giving him Eve in the first place. Eve followed the pattern and blamed the snake for causing them to eat the forbidden fruit. Humans looked to place blame on someone else rather than take responsibility for their actions. It has been this way our entire history. We do not want to be held accountable.

To bring this to today and so that you can directly relate, I am going to ask you to think back over the past week and count up the times you said something similar to the words "Well, it wasn't my fault that didn't work" or "All I know is, I didn't do it, so don't blame me." Did you have at least one of those moments? If you drove a vehicle on the road this past week, the odds are pretty high that a thought like that crossed your mind.

The Truck

Here is a short story about an event that happened to me that shows you how far we will go to blame others for something we did that was wrong. After my wife and I married, it took us a few years to pay back school loans and finally get our own house. When we got married, our two old broken down cars put together would not make one good one. But eventually, we finally got to the point where I bought my first new truck. This truck was my baby! It was a bright red, a 4x4, extended cab truck with the large sport wheels. I washed, waxed, and cleaned that truck and it looked like it just rolled off the showroom floor most of the time. One day we jumped in and went to the local store to buy some mulch and landscaping items. After we had selected the items we wanted, I ran back, jumped in my truck to back up so we could load the heavy items more easily. Without much thought, I put the truck in reverse and backed right into one of those BIG bright yellow bollards. Not only did I back into that big post, it caught the entire back quarter panel bumper and all. I immediately stopped but the major damage was done. What was worse, I had to pull the truck forward from that post just to open the tailgate. Putting my big shinny truck into DRIVE, knowing what was about to be one of the worse scrapping sounds I would ever hear, I pulled forward. I was almost sick. My wife and little son were standing near the truck, and I so much wanted to blame her and ask her why she didn't warn me about the big post, but it wasn't her fault. All she said was, "I am sure glad I wasn't the one that did that." You see, I was the one in the driver's seat. I was the one that put the truck in reverse. I was the one that did not look before I started backing up. It was completely my fault, yet I was looking to blame anyone except me. I remember even telling my wife, "I don't know why they even put these crazy posts out here in the parking lot anyway." That is just how we are today; it is never our fault in our own mind.

As you read earlier in chapter two, the eternal part of our existence has an appointment to keep with Jesus. This appointment is all about what I call your Life in Review. Every act or deed we performed, every word we spoke, every thought that went through our minds has been recorded and will be subject for review. There will be no excuses for any of us when we are called to give an account of our lives to Jesus Christ. You might be thinking, how can that be, some things are just not my fault or you might say, "I didn't know any better." Going back to God's Word, He makes it clear that we have an internal code of ethics hardwired into the fabric of our being so excuses will not be heard. We will look to see just what He says in the following paragraphs and chapters related to this life in review.

God Gave Mankind Responsibility

When God created mankind, He did not just create us to blindly follow His direct orders and for us to wander around with nothing to do. There is an old saying about idle time; it leads to trouble. God gave us a free will because He wanted us to choose to obey Him. Along with the free will came responsibility and accountability for our actions. Notice in the scripture below that the word used in the Bible is dominion, which means to rule over. Being a ruler means responsibility and accountability are both required to adequately perform the job assigned.

So God created man in his own image, in the image
of God created he him; male and female created
he them. And God blessed them, and God said unto
them, Be fruitful, and multiply, and replenish the
earth, and subdue it: and have dominion over the
fish of the sea, and over the fowl of the air, and
over every living thing that moveth upon the earth.
(Genesis 1:27-28)

Your Personal Responsibility

You might be asking yourself, what responsibilities has God given me? The answer to that question is not all that difficult. God has created each one of us with a ministry or a job He wants us to do for Him. I will include just a couple of scriptures that tell us that each one of us has been given gifts that are to be used to do our job for God.

Now there are diversities of gifts, but the same
Spirit. And there are differences of administrations,
but the same Lord. And there are diversities of
operations, but it is the same God which worketh
all in all. But the manifestation of the Spirit is
given to every man to profit withal. For to one is
given by the Spirit the word of wisdom; to another
the word of knowledge by the same Spirit; To
another faith by the same Spirit; to another the
gifts of healing by the same Spirit; To another
the working of miracles; to another prophecy; to
another discerning of spirits; to another divers
kinds of tongues; to another the interpretation of
tongues: But all these worketh that one and the

> *selfsame Spirit, dividing to every man severally as he will.* (1 Corinthians 12:4-11 KJV)

> *Now ye are the body of Christ, and members in particular. And God hath set some in the church, first apostles, secondarily prophets, thirdly teachers, after that miracles, then gifts of healings, helps, governments, diversities of tongues. Are all apostles? are all prophets? are all teachers? are all workers of miracles? Have all the gifts of healing? do all speak with tongues? do all interpret?* (1 Corinthians 12:27-30 KJV)

Yes, you have a job to do for God. He did not create you and me to just be a consumer of oxygen and resources, you are called to do something. The scriptures above also tell us that we will not all do the same job, nor will we all be given the same gifts. In fact, God is pretty clear that we will all be very different. That is what makes our service to God exciting and not boring. When I hear some Christians make a statement like "if you don't do this, or you don't dress a certain way, have this certain gift, then God's spirit isn't living in you." That is a FALSE statement; just look at the words above.

God does not expect us to do the job He has for us without giving us the talent and ability to do that job. That said, it is your responsibility to grow that gift into a mature ministry. God will give you the tools, but it is totally up to you to learn to use them. I will give you a personal example. I learned in my high school days that I like to build things, and I especially liked to do woodworking. We did not have any real woodworking tools on our farm, so the first day I got to go into a real woodshop at school, I was just like a kid in a candy store. I had the raw talent to draw and see objects in 3D, but I had never used those nice power tools, like a table saw, band saw, or a router. Even though I had the talent, I needed to practice using the tools before I could make a nice project. One of the first things you learn in a shop with power tools is SAFETY. My shop teacher was so good and patient, but he knew that I did not know how to safely use these big machines. Our class spent the first six weeks learning safety before we ever cut our first piece of wood. Even though this was so boring, I thank my shop teacher because I still have all of my fingers today.

My first project did not turn out well at all. I wanted to make a small race car, but I wanted mine to be really cool. So I drew it up and started cutting wood. After a pile of sawdust and hours later, my car did not look anything like my drawing, and what was worse, the wheels would not even turn freely. My project was a failure. Had I just given up and quit at that point like so many people do, I would not be making the furniture and toys today from my woodshop at home. I took those raw talents and through years of practice, I learned how to properly use the tools and completed some really nice projects. Do I still make mistakes on my projects? Yes, but I now know how to fix the mistakes and then learn not to repeat them. Most of the wood furniture in our home is hand made by yours truly. My nephews and nieces today love the toys I make. The only negative in this is my wife now does not hesitate to tell me when she wants another piece of furniture. I am a good woodworker because I had the basic raw talent, I learned how to use the right tools, and I practiced on hundreds of projects. Now I really enjoy making things to the point I have passed that talent along to my son. We are supposed to pass along the spiritual maturity we learn to the next generation. I also learned through my many years of woodworking that there are really good tools and there are really bad tools. The use of poor tools will show on your project and it is the same with our spiritual walk, God gives us the best tools, but we have to learn how to use them properly.

I hope, through my personal example, you have learned that our spiritual walk is very similar. God gives us the raw talent, and He even provides the tools, but when we first start, we are "rookies" and we need some training and practice. By the way, we also need to learn some spiritual safety lessons before we even attempt the jobs God has called us to do, like watching the words we say. Understand, you will not convert the entire world to give their lives to Jesus the day after you get saved, so you need to pace yourself and be patient but persistent. God knows we will make mistakes, but He also knows the more we practice and follow His instructions, we will get very good at our spiritual job. So many people today just give up on their walk with God at the first sign of a challenge. We have way too many people today that are just all about the blessing, prosperity, and love. When that doesn't happen in their lives, 100% of the time, they get discouraged and walk away from God. God's Word says that Christians will have problems, trials, and even afflictions, but He also says He will provide help to us during those times. You will learn from your mistakes.

> *Many are the afflictions of the righteous: but the LORD delivereth him out of them all.* (Psalm 34:19 KJV)

To move this discussion along, you might be asking, how do I know what my job is? Your learning of your calling from God begins with a look at yourself. What is it that you are good at? What is it that you really enjoy doing? What is it you do that even if you make a mistake, you will stick with it? If you can pin that down, it is an indicator of what God has created you to do, pointing you in the right direction. Here are just a few examples: are you good with math and numbers? God may want you to be a financial person at your local church or help those that struggle with finances. Can you sing or play an instrument? God may want you leading worship services somewhere or write songs that bring Him glory. Are you good with kids? God may want you helping in a daycare or Sunday school somewhere where you can teach children about Him. Are you a good public speaker? God may want leading small groups in your local church. Can you take complicated things and explain the process so others can understand? God may want you to be a board member or a teacher. This list could go on, but you get the point.

If you have not identified your job God has called you to do, it is YOUR responsibility to be looking for it. The first step in the process is prayer. I am most confident that God just loves it when His children ask Him what He wants us to do. Don't just run out and start trying a bunch of things because that will result in mistakes and failures that may discourage you. Remember, this is the most important thing while you live on this earth so spend time in prayer and be patient. Even when you are pretty sure you know what your job is, it will still take time to develop into that wonderful tool God can use. God is not like the microwave, where everything happens in an instant. God will expect dedication from you even when times are difficult.

I have watched over my lifetime where people have taken those talents God gave them and used them for personal gain. How sad that must make God when people chose not to use their abilities for Him. It is totally your responsibility to identify what God has called you to do and develop those gifts God has given you. Remember, God does not give you bad tools, He gives you the very best but it is up to you to learn to use them safely and properly. God will hold you accountable for how you do this.

How Will We Be Held Accountable?

If you are already a Christian, you should know that God holds us accountable during this life just like our earthly parents. When it came to discipline, did your parents ever say, "this is going to hurt me more than it will hurt you"? I never believed that for a minute! As our heavenly Father, God tells us that along our journey, He will correct us as needed when we disobey Him.

> *And ye have forgotten the exhortation which speaketh unto you as unto children, My son, despise not thou the chastening of the Lord, nor faint when thou art rebuked of him: For whom the Lord loveth he chasteneth, and scourgeth every son whom he receiveth. If ye endure chastening, God dealeth with you as with sons; for what son is he whom the father chasteneth not? But if ye be without chastisement, whereof all are partakers, then are ye bastards, and not sons. Furthermore we have had fathers of our flesh which corrected us, and we gave them reverence: shall we not much rather be in subjection unto the Father of spirits, and live? For they verily for a few days chastened us after their own pleasure; but he for our profit, that we might be partakers of his holiness. Now no chastening for the present seemeth to be joyous, but grievous: nevertheless afterward it yieldeth the peaceable fruit of righteousness unto them which are exercised thereby.* (Hebrews 12:5-11 KJV)

For the time is come that judgment must begin at the house of God: and if it first begin at us, what shall the end be of them that obey not the gospel of God? (1 Peter 4:17 KJV)

Relative to being held accountable, God uses correction during this life and He will also meet with us for a future judgment. Judgment is part of our Christian faith that not many people really want to talk about. The majority of people today have labeled God as this being of true love, and they make statements like "a real loving God will never send anyone to Hell." While He has proven His great love for all of humanity, He also tells us about His justice. Rather than read and find out what God has said on this topic, many remain deceived and unlearned about the fact that we make a choice to believe His words about His love that only comes through Jesus Christ. Each person must do this on our own during this life. We decide how and when we will face God's judgment. God loved us so much that He sent His only Son to come here and live a human life just like us. He lived a sinless life, which is something you and I could never do, and He became a sacrifice to cover our guilt. There is likely none of us that would give up our child to be killed for the guilt of someone else. That is how much God loved us. So when we hear people make these kind of statements that God would not send anyone to Hell, we must understand He already made a way for us to *not go there*, but He leaves the choice completely up to us.

The Lord is not slack concerning his promise, as some men count slackness; but is longsuffering to us-ward, not willing that any should perish, but that all should come to repentance. (2 Peter 3:9 KJV)

Just how will God hold us accountable for how we have lived our lives here on earth? He has told us that our actions are being recorded in "the books" (Rev. 20:12) in Heaven. At the end of our lives, we will individually stand before our Lord to answer His questions as He compares our life record to His requirements. Many people, including Christians today, completely misunderstand how and when God will judge and many even wonder, why must there be judgment? God's word tells us that there are different judgments based upon the records of our individual lives and the fact if you have accepted His Son or not. We will now discuss each of these judgments and how they will apply to us. Before we begin, we will step back and see why there must be a judgment.

Why Judgment?

Judgement is the time for accountability. The first reason there has to be judgment is because God is holy and He, therefore, has to judge disobedience and rebellion. Here is just one scripture that addresses this reason:

> Because it is written, Be ye holy; for I am holy.
> And if ye call on the Father, who without respect
> of persons judgeth according to every man's
> work, pass the time of your sojourning here in
> fear. (1 Pet 1:16-17)

Not only is God holy, His holiness governs the contents of His Kingdom. There will be no disobedience or violation of His laws and statues in His eternal Kingdom. Those who have chosen to willingly disobey Him will be evicted from spending eternity in His Kingdom. That disobedience includes rejection of His Son Jesus as our personal Savior. We cannot say that God did not warn us in advance of the consequences of a decision not to accept His Son.

> *But the fearful, and unbelieving, and the abominable, and murderers, and whoremongers, and sorcerers, and idolaters, and all liars, shall have their part in the lake which burneth with fire and brimstone: which is the second death.* (Revelation 21:8 KJV)

God's Word goes on to tell us the other reason why judgment is needed:

> *For ALL have sinned and come short of the glory of God.* (Romans 3:23)

> *For the wages of sin is death; but the gift of God is eternal life through Jesus Christ our Lord.* (Romans 6:23 KJV)

The Greek word for judgment, as used in Hebrews 9:27 is krisis (kree'-sis), which means decision or justice under divine law. There is a decision point where justice will be applied to each of us when our life here on earth expires. God's own nature dictates that He hold us individually accountable for our decisions, choices, and actions that were done within our free will. Our free will is open to influence from Satan. Satan's entire existence is now to draw as many humans away from God as he can. He does this through lies and deceit. All we have to do is look at the very first sin and how it happened. Satan twisted God's words and planted doubt in the minds of God's creation.

Now the serpent was more subtle than any beast of the field which the LORD God had made. And he said unto the woman, Yea, hath God said, Ye shall not eat of every tree of the garden. And the woman said unto the serpent, We may eat of the fruit of the trees of the garden. (Genesis 3:1-2)

But I fear, lest by any means, as the serpent beguiled Eve through his subtlety, so your minds should be corrupted from the simplicity that is in Christ. (2 Corinthians 11:3)

The serpent was a tool of Satan and placed doubt in Eve's mind. He made her think that God was hiding something. Adam and Eve lost sight of the fact they could eat from all other trees EXCEPT that one, they focused on that tree just like a kid. The result was they believed a LIE. (Genesis 3:4-5, Genesis 2:17)

And when the woman saw that the tree was good for food, and that it was pleasant to the eyes, and a tree to be desired to make one wise, she took of the fruit thereof, and did eat, and gave also unto her husband with her; and he did eat. (Genesis 3:6)

The final action was to commit sin, just like we chose today. The end result was the separation from God and the loss of all innocence.

And they heard the voice of the LORD God walking in the garden in the cool of the day: and Adam and his wife hid themselves from the presence of

the LORD God amongst the trees of the garden.
(Genesis 3:8)

Mankind Becomes Sinners

From the very moment Eve took the first bite of the fruit from the tree, mankind became sinners. There was instant shame on the part of Adam and Eve. God could have destroyed them at that point, but His love was too great. yet He wanted them to account for what they had done. There was fear in Adam and Eve because sin separates us from our loving Father. Sin brought an immediate change between man and God and between man and woman. Because of disobedience, we are all now sinners. God allowed mankind to retain a free choice to obey Him or not. Each person must. at some point, make a choice to accept God's plan to nullify the sin or reject His plan and live in disobedience with no coverage for their sin. We sinned and God made a way out. It is up to us to accept or reject His plan.

For those who make the choice to reject His plan, their actions are building up toward judgment when God will render to every man according to his deeds.

> *But in accordance with your hardness and your impenitent heart you are treasuring up for yourself wrath in the day of wrath and revelation of the righteous judgment of God, who will render to each one according to his deeds.* (Romans 2:5-6)

This is WHY we face JUDGMENT, and this decision we make will determine which judgment will be ours.

The Judgements

To keep this simple, there are several judgments mentioned in scripture but we are going to focus on the two that directly impact us. Each one of us will be at one of these two judgments based upon your choices and actions during your life. What determines which of these two places you will be is if you accepted Jesus Christ as your personal Savior during this life or not. If you did, you will stand before Jesus not so much as your judge, but to review your life's actions. This is commonly referred to as the Judgement Seat of Christ. As a Christian, Jesus died for your sins and once you asked for His forgiveness, these sins are forgotten forever and erased from your record. Jesus blots them out with His blood. If you have rejected God's plan of salvation, you never asked God to forgive you of your sins, and never accepted Jesus Christ as your Savior, then you will be at the Great White Throne Judgement. We will look at these two judgments, so you will understand the difference.

> *And as it is appointed unto men once to die, but after this the JUDGMENT.* (Hebrews 9:27)

The Judgment Seat of Christ

As we discussed back in Chapter 3, this judgment is identified in scripture in 2 Corinthians 5:10. This is the time when all of those that have lived throughout history and have accepted Jesus Christ as their Savior will have a review of their life.

> *For we must all appear before the judgment seat of Christ; that every one may receive the things done in his body, according to that he hath done, whether it be good or bad.* (2 Corinthians 5:10 KJV)

110

*According to the grace of God which is given
unto me, as a wise masterbuilder, I have laid
the foundation, and another buildeth thereon.
But let every man take heed how he buildeth
thereupon. For other foundation can no man
lay than that is laid, which is Jesus Christ. Now if
any man build upon this foundation gold, silver,
precious stones, wood, hay, stubble; Every man's
work shall be made manifest: for the day shall
declare it, because it shall be revealed by fire;
and the fire shall try every man's work of what
sort it is. If any man's work abide which he hath
built thereupon, he shall receive a reward. If any
man's work shall be burned, he shall suffer loss:
but he himself shall be saved; yet so as by fire.*
(1 Corinthians 3:10-15)

This will be a time when Jesus Himself will walk us through
our lives to review all of the things we have done. I ask you,
the reader, to look closely at the description of this judgment.
It says that we will receive of the things done, whether good or
bad. You might be thinking to yourself, what about the sin and
disobedience we committed, will Jesus bring that up? This is
not a time when Jesus will bring up all of our awful sins and
beat us over the head, reminding us of how lost we were. The
reason I believe this to be the case is that Jesus died for the complete forgiveness of our sins. God's word says that when we ask
for forgiveness through our repentance and acceptance of Jesus
that our sins are not only forgiven, they are forgotten never to
be remembered. This is just my personal belief that Jesus will
pull out a big section of our life record that lists all of our sins
and He will show us a big red mark through every page, rip it
up, and burn it. Then He will turn to us and say something like

"I have that covered, now let's talk about what you learned on earth and what my plans are for you in my Kingdom." Again, this is just my thought, you will not find this is the Bible other than the forgiveness part, but what a great way to think about it.

> *As far as the east is from the west, so far hath he removed our transgressions from us.* (Psalm 103:12 KJV)

> *If we confess our sins, he is faithful and just to forgive us our sins, and to cleanse us from all unrighteousness.* (1 John 1:9 KJV)

> *I, even I, am he that blotteth out thy transgressions for mine own sake, and will not remember thy sins,* (Isaiah 43:25 KJV)

This might be when Jesus will point out the times we've wasted where we could have been working for Him and how He wants our full attention in His new kingdom. He might remind us of those talents and abilities He gave us that we just never matured to be used in His service. He might remind us of the many times we didn't go to church, read our Bible, or prayed because we were distracted by life. I think He will want to make sure we understand that He wants us fully devoted to His eternal service.

This will be a wonderful time to spend with our Lord. During this time, Jesus will also give us rewards for our faithfulness. God's word lists several crowns that can be obtained by those that are His children and the scripture above in 2 Corinthians 5:10 says that we will receive of things we have done, and it includes the *good*. You will want to be at this judgment.

The Great White Throne Judgement

This judgment is identified in Revelation 20:11-15. This is the time when all those who are wicked and have rejected God's plan of salvation through His Son will be judged. Notice that this is a judgment, not a life review.

> *And I saw a great white throne, and him that sat on it, from whose face the earth and the heaven fled away; and there was found no place for them. And I saw the dead, small and great, stand before God; and the books were opened: and another book was opened, which is the book of life: and the dead were judged out of those things which were written in the books, according to their works. And the sea gave up the dead which were in it; and death and hell delivered up the dead which were in them: and they were judged every man according to their works. And death and hell were cast into the lake of fire. This is the second death. And whosoever was not found written in the book of life was cast into the lake of fire.* (Revelation 20:11-15 KJV)

You do not want to be at this judgment.

If you are, this means you are eternally lost. It means you will be separated from God and His kingdom because He will not permit any evil into His kingdom. All of those pages of your life book that lists your sin and disobedience will still be there because you never asked Jesus to cover those so they can be removed and forgotten. All of those evils will be played out in front of you like a big movie screen. This will be a time when you will have to be your own lawyer and you will try to make excuses for your disobedience.

This will very likely be one of those times when people will say, "I was a good person," but sadly, that answer will not stand. I also think God may remind you of every time He tried to reach you with a song, a scripture on social media, or a friend who shared the gospel with you. You just laughed it off as a joke. He just might remind you of every time you were more concerned about being politically correct than to stand up for His commandments. Judgment is all about being held accountable for the actions and decisions of your life. How sad it will be for you and for God when He has to say, "Depart from me." I believe there will be a tear in His eye because He loved you so much that His Son died for you.

And you rejected Him.

An Appointment

As we wrap up this chapter, I hope you now have a basic understanding that we are all sinners, and we all require forgiveness. This forgiveness only comes through repentance and acceptance of Jesus in your soul. You should also know that there is a time coming when you and I will stand in judgment by the creator of the universe. It is up to you when and where this happens. Death ends our probationary period. There is no purgatory, no re-incarnation, and no transmigration from one body to another. There will be no second chance to live on earth and get saved, you either die saved or lost.

You and I have an appointment at either the Judgement Seat of Jesus Christ or at the Great White Throne Judgment. Your acceptance of salvation here during this life determines that place and time. There are no exceptions to this inescapable appointment, the choice is all yours. Make the right choice now while you have the opportunity.

> *Dust thou art, and unto dust thou shalt return.*
> (Genesis 3:19)

Other Questions to Consider

- Do you still find yourself blaming others for your mistakes?
- Are you fulfilling the job God has called you to perform?

Chapter 7

A Gap that Only Jesus Christ can Bridge

How many times in our lives have we physically tried to jump over a hole, a puddle of water, or just a gap that we needed to cross only to find out that we couldn't jump that far? When I want a laugh, I go to the internet and search for videos of people (and cats) trying to jump over things or across a gap and they don't make it. As I was growing up, I had a brother who was very much the daredevil on a motorcycle. I saw him many times try to jump a gap and not make it only to crash. I was the smart one and sat by to see if he would make it before I even attempted to make the jump (with age comes wisdom). Not very nice of a big brother, but hey, at that age, I figured he was expendable.

Along this line of thinking, how many of us have tried to build some contraption out of things laying around to span a gap we needed to cross? The Internet is full of pictures of people who stack ladders and poles on non-secure bases, or they want to use a rope, but they tie it off to something flimsy that will never hold their weight. Sometimes we just do not use common sense.

I am telling my age just a little, but I remember the daredevil Evel Knievel. I watched him crash on many of his jumps, but the one that really got my attention was when he tried to jump the Snake River Canyon. I was just smart enough to look at the ramp and the large gap and I knew there was no way he would make it. Of course, he didn't. This is just the way life is so many times. We are faced with huge challenges that we cannot solve on our own. I know guys have a tendency to have just a little too much pride and we feel weak if we have to ask for help. How many times do we fail or get into trouble because we are too proud to ask for help? Relative to being good enough, you should realize by this point in this book that we will never meet the criteria of the creator. The first human beings and all of us since then have created a gap that none of us can bridge. We have created the sin gap by our continued disobedience to God throughout our entire history. The only way that God can allow you and I to cross that sin gap into His eternal Kingdom is if we humble ourselves and ask for His forgiveness.

Building Bridges

Having a mechanical engineering degree, I have always been fascinated with airplane wings and bridges. There is a tremendous amount of education and testing that goes into the design of both. Given the topic of this chapter, I want to focus on the bridge. Some of you reading this book may have attempted to build some type of a structure that would span a gap, so you could cross either on foot or in a vehicle as we discussed above. I am also guessing a few of you out there experienced "structural failure" when your makeshift bridge collapsed. A collapsed bridge likely results in someone getting hurt. It may be funny to watch on the internet, but the price in pain is clearly seen. Yes, I learned the hard way on this topic as a kid on a motorcycle.

I am sure if I would ask the question to you reading this book, "Do you think you could build a bridge?" many of you would answer *yes*. But if I asked you to design and build a bridge that will be used on a major highway, you might not be so quick to say *yes*. Even with a Master's Degree in Mechanical Engineering, I do not have all of the training needed to design a highway approved bridge. In addition to the training, most states require a person designing bridges to have certifications in civil engineering combined with several years of experience before they are allowed to design bridges for our highways.

Man builds some pretty amazing bridges. The long bridge/tunnel in Norfolk, the Golden Gate Bridge, The new bridge near the Hoover Dam, and the one I really like is the high bridge in San Diego that connects Coronado Island to the city. These are some marvels of engineering and construction. There have been bad designs over the years, even though the designers were the best in the business. You can go to YouTube and search for the Tacoma Narrows Bridge and watch what happens to the latest technology at the time being used on a suspension bridge in a windy environment. The Tacoma bridge did not last very long after it was opened. The failure of the bridge was not associated with vehicle traffic at all, it collapsed because the high winds in the area literally tore the bridge apart.

The individuals that design the bridges you drive on are some very smart people, but even the best bridge designer cannot build a bridge to span the great gulf, as Jesus described, that exists between the two eternal destinations. These very smart people have their education and their certifications, but they will never be able to design a bridge to span the separation that man caused between ourselves and God through our disobedience.

The Great Gulf

> *There was a certain rich man, which was clothed in purple and fine linen, and fared sumptuously every day: And there was a certain beggar named Lazarus, which was laid at his gate, full of sores, And desiring to be fed with the crumbs which fell from the rich man's table: moreover the dogs came and licked his sores. And it came to pass, that the beggar died, and was carried by the angels into Abraham's bosom: the rich man also died, and was buried; And in hell he lift up his eyes, being in torments, and seeth Abraham afar off, and Lazarus in his bosom. And he cried and said, Father Abraham, have mercy on me, and send Lazarus, that he may dip the tip of his finger in water, and cool my tongue; for I am tormented in this flame. But Abraham said, Son, remember that thou in thy lifetime receivedst thy good things, and likewise Lazarus evil things: but now he is comforted, and thou art tormented.* (Luke 16:19-25 KJV)

Jesus told this story of the rich man and Lazarus in the book of Luke in which both men die and end up in their eternal destinations. One in torment and the other in Paradise. During this parable, Jesus is pretty clear in His descriptions of these locations for eternal destiny. One destination is a place of beauty and comfort in the presence of God, the other is a place of everlasting pain and torment completely separated from God. Once you have passed from this life, you need to be fully aware that there are only two options; eternity with God or eternity separated from God. You and I will be in one of these two places. Once you are in one of those locations, your eternal residence is final. A very interesting detail Jesus describes in His parable is the "great gulf" that is "fixed" between the two destinations.

> *And beside all this, between us and you there is a great gulf fixed: so that they which would pass from hence to you cannot; neither can they pass to us that would come from thence.* (Luke 16:26)

Jesus Built the Bridge

As we study scripture, we must get into the practice of doing some research to find out the definitions of the words as they are used in a message. Scripture must also be studied with the perspective of the time and situation in which they were written. Applying some study to the parable of the rich man and Lazarus, you will find the Greek word used for *gulf* in Luke 16:26 is *chasma* and it means: an impassable interval. These words of Jesus also tell us that the great gulf is FIXED. That gap is there to stay forever.

God, in His infinite wisdom and knowledge, did provide mankind ONE WAY to cross that gap before we physically die, and that is to repent of our sins and accept Jesus Christ as our Savior. You and I do not have the ability to build a spiritual bridge, nor are we certified to build one. You and I cannot do enough good works during our life to earn and pay the toll to cross that spiritual bridge. Jesus is the ONLY one certified to build the bridge that is required to span the "sin gap" because He paid the toll. God proved His great love for mankind when He sent His Son to die for our sin. Even when we all disobey Him and many completely reject Him, He still sent His Son to die as a sacrifice for each of us on an individual basis. God did that because He wants us to spend eternity with Him, but it is still our choice.

The construction of the bridge that spans the great gulf began when Jesus was born in Bethlehem. That construction continued as Jesus lived a life without sin all the while experiencing a hard life just like you and I must face. Jesus was a carpenter or what I might call today a construction worker, so how more appropriate that He also used the spiritual construction tools of teaching and healing while he was here to show us the way to get to that bridge. Jesus knows what it is like to be a human. When Jesus died and rose again three days later, the spiritual bridge construction was completed and certified.

Jesus was the architect of the spiritual bridge and God's Word tells us the criteria used for its construction. There are two scriptures in the Bible that many Christians today take somewhat out of context because we have become so focused on the well-being of our physical body that we have missed the reason Jesus came and died. As we get older, we begin to physically fall apart and we find we must go to the doctor more frequently as the years go by. Having been in church since before I was even born (my mom carried me to church inside of her), I was always taught that all we have to do is ask God to heal us anytime we wanted and if we had faith, He would heal our physical illness. This teaching is based on several scriptures in the Bible, but there are two verses that I always heard quoted when it came to asking God to heal our bodies. I have included them here:

> *But he was wounded for our transgressions, he was bruised for our iniquities: the chastisement of our peace was upon him; and with his stripes we are healed.* (Isaiah 53:5)

> *Who his own self bare our sins in his own body on the tree, that we, being dead to sins, should*

live unto righteousness: by whose stripes ye were healed. (1 Peter 2:24)

While I do believe that God still works miracles when it comes to healing our physical bodies and I do believe there are times God takes His time to heal us, that is not what these two verses are about. Please pay very close attention to the words of these two scriptures. These verses talk about covering our transgressions, our iniquities, and our sins. I believe these verses tell us He is far more concerned about healing our eternal soul than in healing our physical body. That is why Jesus came and died on the cross to make sure each one of us have a way to heal the eternal spiritual part of our existence. To support this view, Jesus provided some guidance about who we let direct our lives:

And if thy right eye offend thee, pluck it out, and cast it from thee: for it is profitable for thee that one of thy members should perish, and not that thy whole body should be cast into hell. And if thy right hand offend thee, cut it off, and cast it from thee: for it is profitable for thee that one of thy members should perish, and not that thy whole body should be cast into hell. (Matthew 5:29-30)

And fear not them which kill the body, but are not able to kill the soul: but rather fear him which is able to destroy both soul and body in hell. (Matthew 10:28)

God wants our Spirit healed so we can cross the bridge.

You Must Cross that Bridge

God has given each of us a free choice to cross the bridge. We must decide which side of the great gulf we want to spend eternity. I have heard many people say that we can each get to God in our own way and that there are many ways to get to Heaven. NEWS ALERT, no there is not. It does not matter what Hollywood actors say, it does not matter what social media says, it does not matter what your favorite political party says, and it does not even matter what some preachers are speaking from the pulpits of today's church. God's Word makes it very clear there is one way and one way only to enter His Kingdom. That way is through Jesus Christ. You and I cannot just walk up to that bridge and stroll across without a change to our lives. Jesus is standing at the entrance of that bridge and He requires us to accept Him as our savior. Jesus paid the toll for us, and He has to be the one to allow us entrance to the bridge. Before He allows us to even get on the bridge, we must repent of our sins and confess Him as our savior. Only then can we get on the bridge.

> *Jesus saith unto him, I am the way, the truth, and the life: no man cometh unto the Father, but by me.* (John 14:6)

> *Because strait is the gate, and narrow is the way, which leadeth unto life, and few there be that find it.* (Matthew 7:14)

You and I cannot build the bridge to heaven, nor can we even go across it without repenting of our sins and letting the light of Jesus shine from within our Spirit. If we could be good enough on our own works or by the multiple ways we hear about today, then Jesus would not have had to come to earth and die for our sins. The fact God sent Jesus to earth to die for our sins is proof there is only one way to cross the bridge over the great gulf. I love the song I heard on the radio not long ago, "What a Strange Way to Save the World."

There is only one master bridge builder that has constructed the path for our eternal spiritual journey and that is Jesus Christ.

Chapter 8

Do You Think You are Good Enough?

For by grace are ye saved through faith; and that not of yourselves: it is the gift of God: Not of works, lest any man should boast. (Ephesians 2:8-9 KJV)

My mother took teaching her kids about Jesus to a whole new level. I remember as a kid, she was always talking about God and I really believe she invented the phrase "what would Jesus do?" before it became popular on T-shirts and license plates! My mom just went above and beyond when it came to putting into practice the words in Proverbs 22:6 that says, "Train up a child in the way he should go: and when he is old, he will not depart from it." She would draw up little cartoons and put a scripture verse on those cartoons then place them all over the house in the most inconspicuous places. There are certain verses of scripture I remember to this day because of those verses around the house. Would you have a guess where she put Philippians 4:13? Yes, on the bathroom door facing the toilet (water closet for you prim and proper types). If you don't know that verse, it is "I can do all things through Christ which strengthens me." Needless to say, I never had to use a laxative.

That basically describes my early childhood home life and the fact that I was always under the influence of God's hand, but like most young kids, I didn't listen. I thought I was good enough. If you remember my story as a kid from chapter 1 and how I was good compared to my buddies and because I "got saved" at the age of ten, I finally learned I was only fooling myself. Now comes the rest of the story.

It took me many years to finally get the message that I needed to get a real relationship with Jesus, not just a religion where I went to church every Sunday. For many of you out there who can relate to a similar story, I can tell you that God does have His hand of guidance on our lives when others pray for us. That was never clearer than just a few months before I graduated from high school, my grandfather (yes, the Baptist minister) asked me what I was going to do with my life. Even just a few months from graduating, I had given no thought to my future. He knew I made pretty good grades in school so he told me I needed to become an engineer since I was good at math. Mind you that I had not even taken the SAT exam, nor had I applied to any college for entrance. He personally set up a meeting with the dean of the engineering school, and we had an on-the-spot interview. I remember quite clearly how the dean looked at me and asked, "If I let you in this school, will you make it through to graduation?" I, of course, said *yes*.

You might be asking what does this have to do with God's plan and who defines good? Here is the part that shows how God moves in our lives. This university was a private university which equates to "very expensive." My family was poor to say the least, and I had already missed all of the scholarships, so it was up to me to pay if I were to attend college. To bring this to a close, God made a way where, I can tell you, there was no way. As I look back today, I still cannot figure how I got into that school, how I paid for it, and how I made it through. It had to be God.

Here is the best part of my story. Psalms 37:23 says, "The steps of a good man are ordered by the Lord; and He delighteth in his way. Though he fall, he shall not be utterly cast down; for the Lord upholdeth him with his hand." That is exactly what happened to me. My full intent was to move away from home, and never really return. I had no intention of going to church, I was on my own and I was going to live the college lifestyle. Needless to say, God had other plans.

On my very first day after moving in, I met my new roommate. We were complete strangers prior to this day. It was the weekend before the first day of classes and it was a Sunday morning. I thought this was going to be my first Sunday to sleep in since mom always made me go to church. Did I have a rude awakening? As you remember from earlier that my roommate woke me up the first day and asked me about going to church. That is just how God works, folks! Then something even more amazing happened, that little voice I heard when I was ten that I had since ignored for years, came back into my ears. So, I went and that was the first step in the right direction back to God.

Following that church service, my roommate asked me to go to a meeting with a group of college students called Outward Bound. It is there I met the most fantastic group of young people that really knew what it meant to follow Jesus. The rest is history. Oh, my bad attitude... God miraculously took it away, and I didn't even realize it until one day I heard someone using foul language, and it pierced my heart like a knife. God healed me, spiritually. Never before had foul language bothered me so much. I knew something inside my life had changed. You might say that it is pretty simple, but it was the very clear sign that Jesus was working on me from the inside out. He knew I needed help; He gave it to me through this wonderful group of college students and His forgiveness for my years of ignoring His call on my life.

For every student, college ends all of a sudden. One day you are on campus going to class and taking tests and the next day, you are part of the real world whether you like it or not. The world has a cruel way of saying, "Welcome newbie!" We all typically follow similar paths in that we realize we must begin to take on responsibility, which includes a job, a family, a home, cars, etc. At times we can quickly become overwhelmed and we let our daily life completely consume our time. If you are like me, my real world life began to consume all of my time, leaving very little for my spiritual well-being. After a while, I become numb to my responsibility to give any of my time to God and I neglected my spiritual walk. I was still going to church and doing the "work of the Lord," but I was just going through the motions. My job, my sport, my hobbies, my house, and my life, in general, had come to rule my time. My spiritual life paid the price.

I was very active in our local church and I never did anything really bad in the eyes of the world. I became a very respected and successful businessman but something was missing. I just couldn't enjoy much satisfaction in all that I was accomplishing.

Fast forward to the end of my Engineering business career to my recent retirement. I was pretty much one of those super health nuts that didn't drink alcohol, didn't smoke, didn't do drugs, tried to eat healthy, and boy did I exercise. I would ride thousands of miles on my bicycle every year. I would train and participate in marathon distance events and did I ever enjoy it. I really never went to a doctor except in really bad cases of a cold, which was very infrequent. Right near my retirement date, I began to experience serious health issues. Within months of my retirement, my health issues grew worse as there were times that I would nearly pass out for absolutely no reason. My digestive system seemed like it was revolting but there was no pattern. I am sure it had to do with eating all of those White Castle hamburgers. After three years of these symptoms, I could no longer safely go cycling nor could I do those high-intensity workout sessions. I was beginning to get extremely frustrated because all of the things I was looking forward to doing in my retirement were beginning to vanish.

My symptoms grew worse and, as you might expect, I started going to numerous doctors. I visited gastroenterologists, cardiologists, and neurologists. I had so many tests run I lost count. The surprise to me was the results from every test came back indicating there was absolutely nothing wrong with me and in fact, I was in better health than 85% of the people my age. The symptoms continued to the point I finally contacted one of the nation's premier hospitals. They accepted me as a patient and I spent a week in their facility, seeing doctors and running tests. At the end of the week, they came back and, in essence, told me what I had been told so many times that I was super healthy. Their diagnosis was that I was experiencing Persistent Postural-Perceptual Dizziness (PPPD), which is where you become hypersensitive to certain types of motion that in turn throws off your vestibular system causing dizziness and nausea. The treatment was simple physical therapy. I left the hospital excited that I at least had an answer and a new hope that, within a few weeks, I would be back to normal. I felt a new breath of life.

Unfortunately, after the recommended length of treatments with the physical therapist, the treatments did not seem to be resolving my illness. I grew even more frustrated than ever. I was pulling into the parking lot of the physical therapist office to go in for my last treatment with little hope I was ever going to get better. I was fifteen minutes early for this last appointment. As I pulled into the lot, a song came on our local Christian radio station by Natalie Grant titled, "More than Anything." I had heard the song a few times before, but like so many times we just hear a song and do not listen to the words and the message. I am sure God planned that moment. It was quiet, I was alone with the world outside, and feeling pretty down. The words to that song hit me like a ton of bricks. I finally realized that for much of my adult life and especially the last three years, I had been asking God to heal me of this illness and questioning why He didn't. The words to that song opened my eyes to realize that this life is not about me, my physical body, or the "good deeds" I was doing at our local church. As I had for much of my life, I was going through the motions of serving God without knowing God at the deepest level and allowing His Holy Spirit to work inside of me. I was still trying to solve my problems on my own.

I have been and continue to be a Sunday school teacher for over thirty-five years. I would get up every Sunday morning and teach a lesson about Jesus Christ, yet I finally realized that I was not as close to Him on a personal level like I should be. Yes, I was still saved, but I was not giving my all to God like I should have. He had blessed me so much, yet I was not dedicating the time to my spiritual walk that God wanted. The song I mentioned above says, "Help me want the healer more than the healing." It was right then that God got my attention. I had placed all of my focus on me rather than on service to the only one that is really good enough. All of my work in the church, all of my giving of tithes, all of my Sunday School lessons were "good", but they were not going to get me to Heaven. I realized that I have to want Jesus more than anything regardless of my physical health or any situation that I put before Him. It took me three and a half years to finally listen to God. Boy, am I hard-headed.

Did God physically heal me? Not yet. God does not promise His children a life of complete luxury and no problems like some people claim today. In fact, David wrote in the book of Psalms (34:19 KJV), "Many are the afflictions of the righteous: but the LORD delivereth him out of them all." God knows best how to get our attention and what it will take to keep us focused on serving Him. A majority of my life was dedicated to staying in shape, doing marathon distance bike riding, martial arts, weightlifting and cardio work. I look back now and I see all of those hours I spent using me-time that could have been used in service to God. Please do not take me wrong, God's word says our body is the temple of God and we are supposed to take care of it, but not to the extreme I had taken it.

I always struggled with a few verses in the Book of Matthew when Jesus was talking about plucking out your eye or cutting off your hand. Those verses seemed strange that Jesus would tell us that we might have to go to such an extreme to serve Him. Matthew 5:30 (KJV) says, "And if thy right hand offend thee, cut it off, and cast it from thee: for it is profitable for thee that one of thy members should perish, and not that thy whole body should be cast into hell". Going through these physical challenges for a long time has brought clarity to me about what Jesus was saying. You see, I know that if God healed me, I would be right back out there for hours every week whipping this now almost sixty-year-old body into shape on the bike and in the gym. All that effort might make me look a little better in a casket someday, but it will not get me closer to God or doing His work. God cares more about me spending eternity with Him in Heaven than He does for me to "feel really good" for a few years here on earth. God knows me better than I know myself. With you, it may be some hobby, activity, job, or a person, but we cannot let anything come between us and our eternal destination if we want that destination to be Heaven.

I am only telling this story of my life because I know there are so many people attending churches across the world that are doing the same thing I was doing and being deceived by Satan that we are on our way to Heaven because of all the good works we are doing. We go to church all of our lives, we do good works, we look the part, and we play the part of a Christian, but we are not allowing the light of Christ shine as brightly as it should from inside of us. Jesus tells us in His own words that we are the light of the world. That light is Jesus. I am just like everyone else; I am not good enough. Only Jesus' light inside of me makes me an acceptable resident in His eternal kingdom. That light cannot shine unless it is inside of our spirit. I pray anyone that reads this book finds guidance to arrive at truly loving Jesus Christ.

Nothing you and I can do will ever earn the right to enter God's Kingdom. But, once we finally admit to God we have sinned and we have asked for His forgiveness, we belong to Him. God's

Word tells us, in 1 John 1:9 (KJV), If we confess our sins, he is faithful and just to forgive us our sins, and to cleanse us from all unrighteousness. You might take the information so far in this book and think that since God says He will forgive me and that I cannot do enough good work to get into heaven on my own, I can just go out and continue to live any way I want. That is not the case. I once heard a statement that explains why Christians are still required to obey God, keep His commandments, and do good works that I think you should read. It goes something like this: It is true we cannot do enough good works to ever cover our debt of sin, only Jesus can do that. But once we do accept Him into our lives, He wants us doing those good works so that those around us will see a difference, which in turn will allow us to make a difference in the lives of everyone that crosses our path. That is how we can share His love with those around us.

Don't let those attending your funeral say you were just a good person, let them say you were a child of the King.

Other Questions to Consider

- Are you giving God 100%?
- How can we avoid getting wrapped up in life and ourselves?
- Are you continuing to obey His Commandments while you perform your Christian calling?

Conclusion

*That if thou shalt confess with thy mouth the
Lord Jesus, and shalt believe in thine heart that
God hath raised him from the dead, thou shalt
be saved. For with the heart man believeth unto
righteousness; and with the mouth confession is
made unto salvation. (Romans 10:9-10)*

While this is a short and simple book, I pray that the content and some of the experiences I have shared will help you find your way to being the person God wants you to be when compared to His standard of measure for being good. As you have read through this book, you can see that there have been many "good" influences on my life from people who God has placed in my path. Each of us needs to know that as a Christian, we are here to share the hope of the Gospel of Jesus Christ with all those we meet. I wonder what would have happened in my life if those influences had not been listening to the guidance of the Holy Spirit when it came to sharing with me. Each of you can be a positive influence on someone's life.

Being good does not get you a ticket to cross the bridge into Heaven. We cannot be good enough on our own. We cannot compare ourselves to those around us, but we must compare ourselves to the lifestyle God has told us about in His word. Only accepting Jesus Christ as your Savior will make you good enough to enter His eternal kingdom. Once you have accepted Him, He does expect us to live by the Moral code He has written upon our hearts. Jesus said in John 14:15, "If you love Me, keep My commandments."

> *For by grace are ye saved through faith; and that not of yourselves: it is the gift of God: Not of works, lest any man should boast. For we are his workmanship, created in Christ Jesus unto good works, which God hath before ordained that we should walk in them.* (Ephesians 2:8-10)

You now have the information you need to make an eternal decision. You now can have hope for an eternal life because we know God made a plan to cover our sins. We in ourselves cannot nor will we ever be good enough to enter God's Kingdom. But, Jesus paid the price to cover our sin-stained lives and provides us access to live with Him forever.

Why do I believe this? Because Jesus has offered us hope through the promise of His soon return. I have come to learn that when Jesus makes a promise, I am most confident it will come to pass. Here is His promise:

> *And while they looked steadfastly toward heaven as he went up, behold, two men stood by them in white apparel; Which also said, Ye men of Galilee, why stand ye gazing up into heaven? this same Jesus, which is taken up from you into heaven, shall so come in like manner as ye have seen him go into heaven.* (Acts 1:10-11 KJV)

Let not your heart be troubled: ye believe in God, believe also in me. In my Father's house are many mansions: if it were not so, I would have told you. I go to prepare a place for you. And if I go and prepare a place for you, I will come again, and receive you unto myself; that where I am, there ye may be also. (John 14:1-3 KJV)

I want to conclude this book with the same question we started, where will you be the day after you die? Now do you think you are good enough on your own? Make sure of your eternal destination before that day arrives. While it may not be in your phone calendar, your appointment to meet Jesus has been scheduled.

Last Question to Consider

- What if that day is tomorrow? Author Biography

Scott Johnson was born and currently resides in southern Indiana. Now retired, he spent over 37 years in support of the Department of Defense as an engineering leader and senior manager. With a Master's Degree in Engineering and a Public Administration, Scott has many years of experience working with a wide variety of business and personal topics. He is a martial arts instructor and serves as the adult Sunday school teacher at Grace Full Gospel Church with 35 years of teaching experience. Scott is married to his wife of 35 years Paula and has one son Matthew.

Author Biography

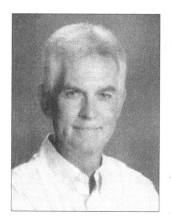

Scott Johnson was born and currently resides in southern Indiana. Now retired, he spent over 37 years in support of the Department of Defense as an engineering leader and senior manager. With a Master's Degree in Engineering and a Public Administration, Scott has many years of experience working with a wide variety of business and personal topics. He is a martial arts instructor and serves as the adult Sunday school teacher at Grace Full Gospel Church with 35 years of teaching experience. Scott is married to his wife of 35 years Paula and has one son Matthew.

CPSIA information can be obtained
at www.ICGtesting.com
Printed in the USA
LVHW041042150920
666055LV00004B/442